ZERO HOUR

THE ANZACS ON THE WESTERN FRONT

LEON DAVIDSON

TEXT PUBLISHING MELBOURNE AUSTRALIA

The paper used in this book is manufactured only from wood grown in sustainable regrowth forests.

The Text Publishing Company
Swann House
22 William Street
Melbourne Victoria 3000
Australia
textpublishing.com.au

First published by The Text Publishing Company 2010
Reprinted 2010, 2011 (twice)

Cover design by W. H. Chong
Text design by Susan Miller
Typeset in Garamond by J&M Typesetting
Printed and bound by Griffin Press

Cover image: AWM E05988A: 'Over the top'. A composite photograph, originally known as 'A hop over', constructed by Captain Frank Hurley, an Official War Photographer.

Other images, opposite page 1: AWM E00825 Soldiers of the 45th Battalion wearing gasmasks in a trench in the Ypres sector. Pages 6, 43, 73, 103, 136, 176: AWM E00700 A scene on the Menin road beyond Ypres. Pages 22, 57, 90, 121, 160, 197: AWM E00103 Two members of the 8th Battalion manning a trench in the Somme region. At the time German troops were located 275 metres away.

All Alexander Turnbull Library images are from the Royal New Zealand Returned and Services' Association Collection.

National Library of Australia
Cataloguing-in-Publication data:

Davidson, Leon, 1973–

Zero hour: the Anzacs on the Western Front/Leon Davidson.

ISBN: 9781921656071 (pbk.)

For secondary school age.

Australia. Army. Australian and New Zealand Army Corps—History. World War, 1914–1918—Australia. World War, 1914–1918—Campaigns—Western Front.

940.40994

AWARDS FOR LEON DAVIDSON

Zero Hour

SHORTLISTED

2011 CBCA Awards, Eve Pownall Award for Information Books

FINALIST

2011 New Zealand Post Children's Book Awards, Non-Fiction

Scarecrow Army

WINNER

2006 CBCA Awards, Eve Pownall Award for Information Books
2006 New Zealand Post Book Awards, Non-Fiction

FINALIST

Elsie Locke Award
2006 Library & Information Association New Zealand
Aotearoa Children's Book Awards

Red Haze

WINNER

Elsie Locke Award
2007 Library & Information Association New Zealand
Aotearoa Children's Book Awards

HONOUR BOOK

2007 CBCA Awards, Eve Pownall Award for Information Books

FINALIST

2007 New Zealand Post Book Awards, Non-Fiction

Leon Davidson grew up with Second World War comics and movies and tried to enlist in the New Zealand Armed Forces when he was eight. After studying Classics, he spent ten years overseas, mainly in Melbourne. He now works as a primary school teacher in Wellington.

TO MY GRANDFATHER
JACK DAVIDSON
AND MY GREAT-GRANDFATHER
JOHN ERRINGTON

CONTENTS

UNITED
KINGDOM
Dover
English Channel
Nieuport
Yser River
FLANDERS
Passchendaele
Ypres
Messines
Hazebrouck
Armentières
Fleurbaix
Étaples
Fromelles
Loos
Mons
Vimy
Arras
Bullecourt
Le Quesnoy
Cambrai
Bapaume
Somme River
SOMME
Montbrehain
Albert
Péronne
Dernancourt
Amiens
Le Hamel
Villers-
Bretonneux
FRANCE
Chemin des Dames
Reims
Chantilly
Seine River
Paris
Western Front 1914
Western Front 1918
0
10
20
30 miles
0
10
20
30
40
50 kilometres

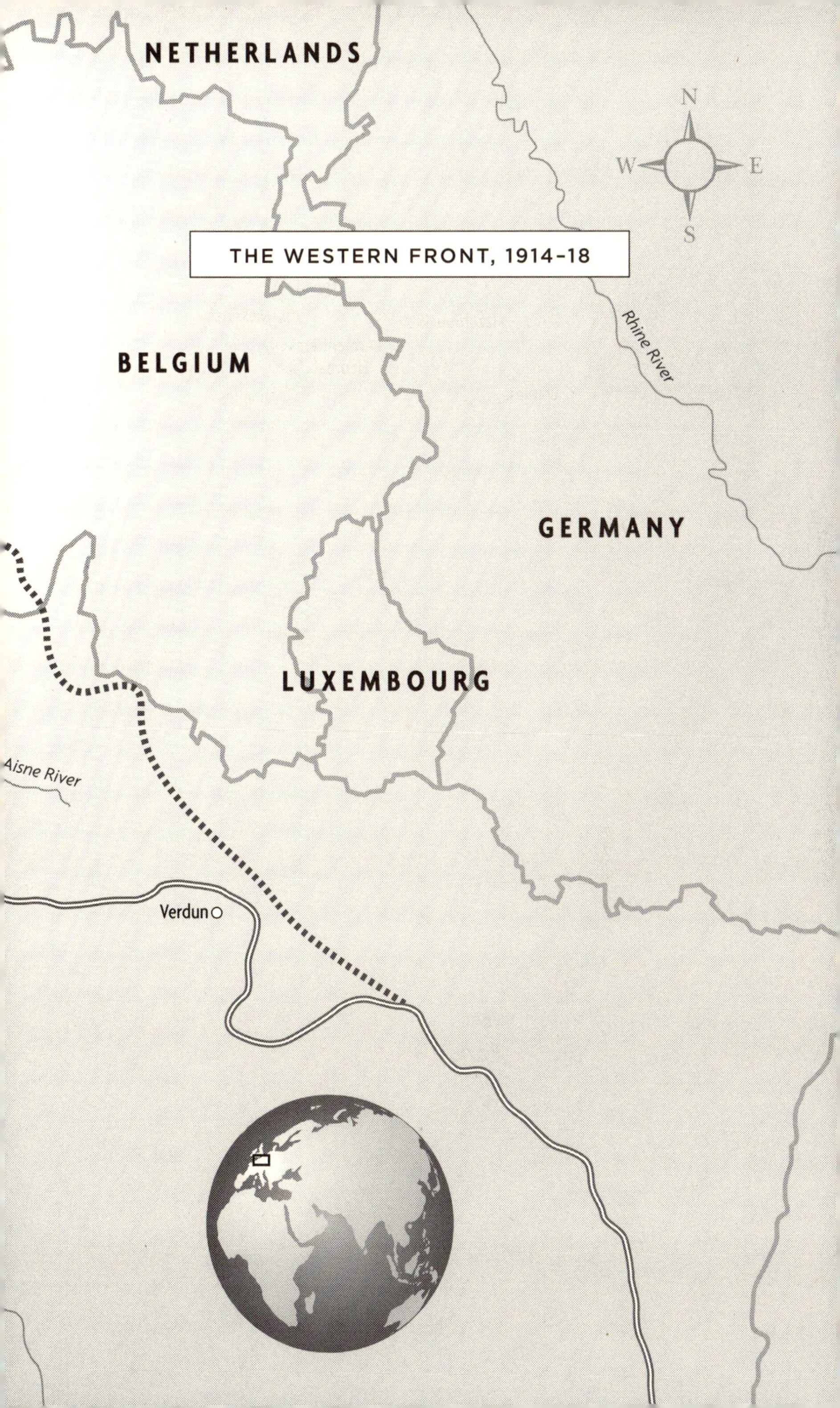
NETHERLANDS
N
W
E
S
THE WESTERN FRONT, 1914–18
Rhine River
BELGIUM
GERMANY
LUXEMBOURG
Aisne River
Verdun

INTRODUCTION

DARK, COLD MORNINGS. Anzac Day. Old men marched or wheeled slowly past, with rows of medals pinned to their suits. When I was a child, they were from another world, like the stone memorial bridge in my hometown.

At home, I had a thick book about the First World War. There were pictures of villages with brick buildings and a church. Below each was a photo of the same village, crumbled and smashed. I remember a painting of a driver holding the head of a dying horse to keep it out of the mud, and cartoons of men in long coats, bent over a brazier, with rain pelting down. There were names too—Messines, Passchendaele, Ypres and the Somme.

As I got older, I noticed portraits of men in uniform hanging on the walls of other people's houses. I heard stories of uncles gassed and grandfathers shot. I learned that my own great-grandfather had fought in the Great War, but even though I'd been to Anzac Day parades, I knew nothing of what he'd lived through. So I started reading about the New Zealand Rifle Regiment he served in, and his journey through that unknown world.

The sheer size and tragedy of the Western Front campaign are difficult to comprehend. In four years, over 3 million soldiers were killed and 11 million wounded. In the small, mediaeval village of Ypres, Belgium, 56,000 names, including those of over 6000 Australians, are carved into its walls. Every night, buglers pay their respects to the fallen by playing the Last Post. Another memorial at the Somme records over 10,000 Australians, while seven memorials around Belgium and France name more than 4000 New Zealanders, who, by the end of the war, were missing, men with no known graves, men who were blown to pieces or swallowed by mud. These are just some of the war's missing.

Zero Hour is about the New Zealanders and Australians on the Western Front, but, even so, it's not the whole story. The hardest thing about writing this book was deciding what to leave out. I wanted to tell the story of the war and give a sense of what it was like for the soldiers—those men who enlisted to fight until they were killed or wounded, or until the war ended.

In New Zealand and Australia, we tend to focus on the 1915 eight-month Gallipoli campaign—our 'baptism of fire'—at the expense of our much longer and bloodier involvement on the Western Front. We shouldn't. For 32 months on the Western Front the Australians and New Zealanders endured the heaviest bombardments in history. They were gassed, drowned in mud, fought beside tanks and stormed village strongholds. It was here that the fighting forces of Australia and New Zealand came of age, here that they gained the reputation of 'shock troops', here that they grew to believe they were as good as the British troops if not better than them. It was here too that men raised on stories of Mother England and the Empire, realised that their own countries were better places to live.

'I personally feel', said Private Sidney Stanfield, at the age of 87, 'that by lionising Gallipoli...they do overlook the severity of the fighting and the extent of the suffering on the Western Front...Seven months on Gallipoli versus three years on the Western Front. There's quite a difference, isn't there?'

Zero hour was the name given to the moment of each attack. As their officers' watches ticked towards it, each soldier faced his fate on the other side of the sandbags. Some met their death, others went on to brave another zero hour, and another.

For me, zero hour also says something about the extraordinary time these men lived and died in. The old world of steam engines and horse-drawn wagons was being replaced by new technology which enabled war on a scale that had never been imagined before; war fought with tanks and aeroplanes, rapid-firing guns and chemical weapons. As these men fought to defend their known world, the world itself was changing around them.

THE AUSTRALIAN AND NEW ZEALAND DIVISIONS OF I ANZAC CORPS AND II ANZAC CORPS:

1st Australian Division (1st Division)
2nd Australian Division (2nd Division)
3rd Australian Division (3rd Division)
4th Australian Division (4th Division)
5th Australian Division (5th Division)
New Zealand Division

Artillery in action in Belgium.
Alexander Turnbull Library G- 13029-1/2

BRITISH AND COMMONWEALTH ARMIES

SECTION: 8–10 men, commanded by a sergeant or corporal.

PLATOON: four sections, 30–60 men, commanded by a lieutenant.

COMPANY: four platoons, around 200 men, commanded by a captain or major.

BATTALION: four companies, around 1000 men—including cooks, wagon drivers, medical personnel, stretcher-bearers, and a trench mortar battery—commanded by a lieutenant colonel.

INFANTRY BRIGADE: four battalions, between 2500 and 5000 troops, commanded by a brigadier general.

DIVISION: three infantry brigades, three artillery brigades, four engineer companies, mortar batteries, a machine-gun battalion and pioneer battalion—10,000 to 20,000 troops, commanded by a major general.

CORPS: two or more divisions, commanded by a lieutenant general.

ARMY: two or more corps, commanded by a general.

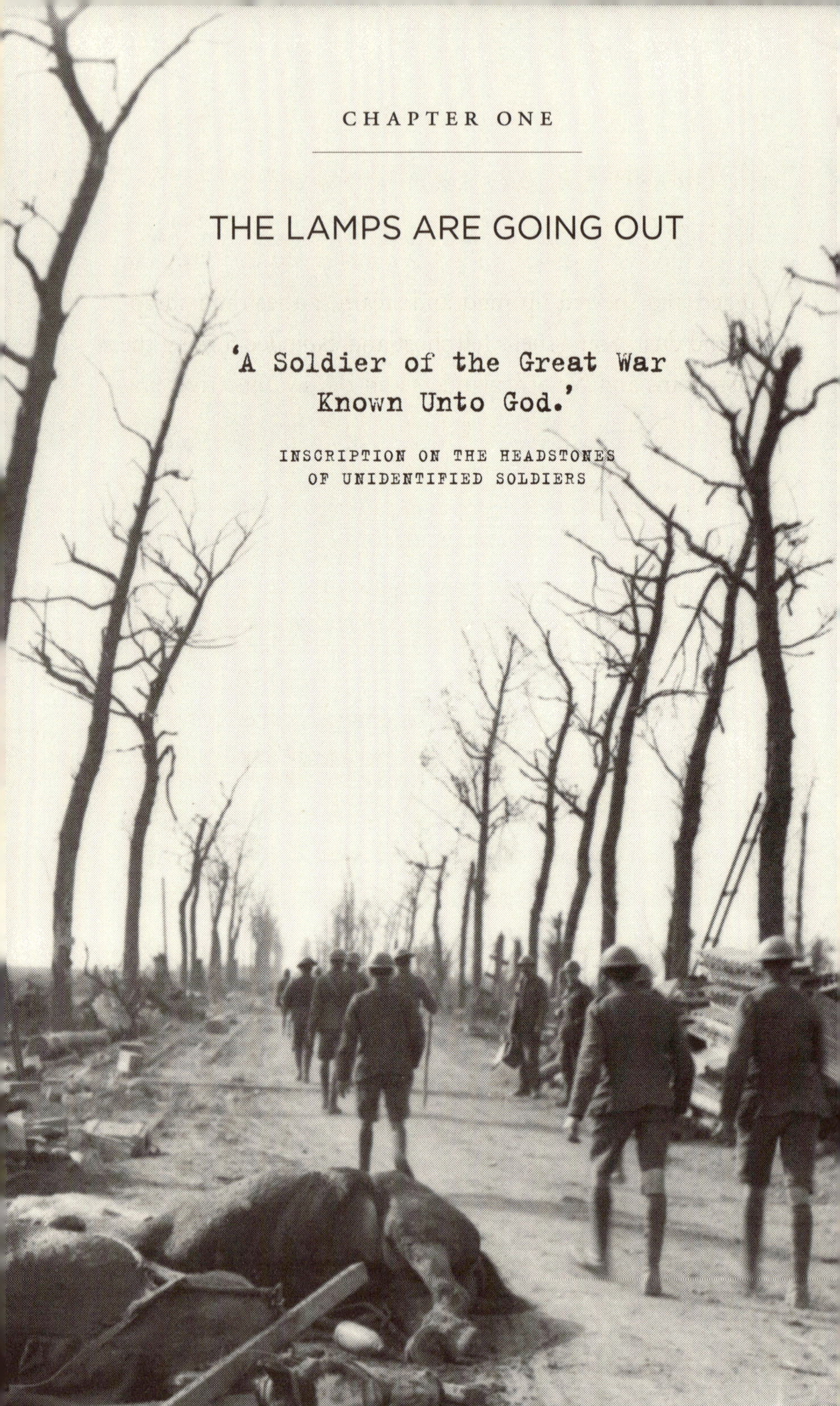

CHAPTER ONE

THE LAMPS ARE GOING OUT

'A Soldier of the Great War
Known Unto God.'

INSCRIPTION ON THE HEADSTONES
OF UNIDENTIFIED SOLDIERS

AT ZERO HOUR, 5.25 a.m., the artillery opened fire. The creeping barrage of exploding shells was meant to give the men cover and maim the Germans but it was thin and ragged and spewed up mud and steam, rather than shrapnel and dust. Some shells fell short and exploded among the Australians and New Zealanders and the swampy river and mud slowed them down. But the Diggers still advanced.

The Germans waited, their guns silent. They knew the attack was coming—a Scottish deserter had told them—so the commanders had put their elite Jaeger troops with extra machine guns into the line. Each machine gun could shoot 500 bullets a minute, and as the Diggers came into sight, the Germans fired. Wounded men slumped into the swamp or water-swollen shell holes and drowned. Private Leonard Hurse had begged to take part after being selected to stay behind. As he ploughed through the mud he turned to Lance Corporal Ernest Williams, bellowing, 'I wouldn't have missed this for a thousand.' He was shot through the head. The following wave filled the gaping holes in the line, passing the wounded and dead. The cratered slope was too slippery to charge, so they slithered forward from shell hole to shell hole, their clothes weighed down by mud.

As more men got close to the dense, uncut belts of wire, they unclogged their guns and rifles and looked for ways through. One group charged into a gap across a sunken road that led to Passchendaele, but it was a trap, and they were gunned down.

It was 12 October 1917, over three years since the Great

War had started, and the Australians and New Zealanders were now considered crack troops. They'd been put into the centre of the attack to capture Bellevue Spur and Passchendaele, near Ypres, Belgium, and were charged with securing the most vital objectives in an offensive that the British commanders believed could bring the war's end closer. But men kept dying in their thousands, and the war, which many had expected to last six months, just kept going.

1914

The Great War, or the 'war to end all wars', was triggered by the assassination of Archduke Franz Ferdinand, heir to the Austrian throne, by a Serbian on 28 June 1914. At first, no one expected a single death to lead to a world war, but tensions in Europe had been building for decades. Old empires wanted to maintain their power while new countries wanted a share of the world's resources.

On one side the Allies were lined up: Britain, France and Russia. On the other side were Germany and Austria–Hungary.

On 28 July, Austria began bombarding the Serbian capital. The Austrians had the backing of Germany, which saw an opportunity to break the growing military power of Russia and France. Russia, which had its own links to Serbia, declared war on Austria. As France called up its army, Germany declared war on both Russia and France and launched the Schlieffen Plan: to knock the French out of the war before Russia had fully mobilised its massive army.

THE SCHLIEFFEN PLAN

Despite having over 1.5 million soldiers on the French borders, the Germans knew that the heavily defended French forts would be too formidable to pass. Instead, 320,000 German troops would march into neutral Belgium, overrun the 84,000-strong Belgian Army, then sweep down into France and circle in behind Paris. The manoeuvre was meant to take six weeks. Paris was to be captured, trapping the French troops between the city and the border. With France's surrender, General Helmuth von Moltke would be able to shift his troops to face the Russians.

The German Kaiser, Wilhelm II, knew the invasion of Belgium would bring Britain into the war, but he and his generals had little respect for the 80,000-strong British force. He referred to them as a 'contemptible little army' and expected to roll over them as easily as the Belgians.

The Germans invaded Belgium on 4 August. Britain declared war on Germany that night. The Great War had started.

GOD SAVE THE KING

On the other side of the world, people in Australia and New Zealand closely followed the events in Europe. The two countries were part of the vast British Empire, and saw Britain, their major trading partner, as the 'mother country'. Even those not born there were raised on stories about British conflicts—the Battle of Waterloo and the Crimean War—and sang 'God Save the King'. If Britain was defeated, they not only faced being alone in the Pacific, they also risked becoming German colonies.

When New Zealand and Australian politicians immediately offered 'the last man and last shilling' to defend Britain, people in both countries took to the streets, waving the Union Flag and singing patriotic songs.

Most people welcomed the war, and as soon as the recruiting offices opened men queued to volunteer. Initially only men aged between 19 and 38 were accepted, so some simply lied about their age while others got permission from their parents. Eighteen-year-old Sergeant Henry 'Harry' Kahan was accepted after his mum wrote a note saying it was okay. Older men shaved their faces to look younger and some who were rejected tried their luck again in a different city. One man travelled from Adelaide to Hobart to Sydney before being accepted.

In cities, men gave up their jobs as teachers, policemen or office clerks, while in the country, bush-clearers and farmhands travelled to the nearest recruitment station. One New Zealander sold a horse he'd stolen to pay his way to the nearest station. Some farmers simply locked their gates, not knowing when they'd return.

The men, who were mainly single, volunteered for many reasons—to see the world, for the adventure, to defeat the 'barbaric' Germans, to escape unhappiness, to see the 'mother country', or to fight for the English King, the British Empire, and their own country. Others needed a job, and the army was paying five shillings a day for the New Zealanders and six for the Australians. Some men just went because their mates were going.

At military camps the men—20,000 Australians and 8000 New Zealanders—put their full effort into training. No one wanted to be left behind and miss out on what was going to be a short war. With the new artillery and rapid-firing guns, many people believed it would be over by Christmas, six months away. Sir Edward Grey, the British foreign secretary didn't share that view. 'The lamps are going out all over Europe,' he wrote. 'We shall not see them lit again in our lifetime.'

The Australian and New Zealand forces were offered to the British Army to use however and wherever its commanders saw fit, although both countries were responsible for the men's food, transport, clothing, wages and even ammunition. Despite their pay being below the minimum wage, the Australians were the highest paid soldiers in the war. They became known as 'six bob a day tourists'. British troops would come to hate going into towns that the Australians and New Zealanders had been in; their one-shilling pay wasn't enough to cover what the locals expected.

'THE CONTEMPTIBLES'

The small Belgian Army momentarily slowed the German advance at its borders but was forced into retreat. When Belgian civilians took up arms to defend their homeland, the Germans dragged young and old from their houses and killed them without trial—by the end of the war over

5000 civilians had been executed. In one mediaeval town, they burned down buildings dating from 1425. As masses of refugees fled the advancing army, stories were printed in newspapers around the world about atrocities committed by 'barbaric monsters' against the 'poor people' of Belgium.

The Belgian resistance gave the British time to get their 80,000 troops, under the command of Field Marshal Sir John French, across the English Channel. On 23 August, in Mons, Belgium, the British held off 160,000 German troops for six hours. When news reached them that the defeated French forces on their right were pulling back and that the Belgian Army on their left had retreated, they were forced into a fighting withdrawal.

After a two-week, 190-kilometre retreat to the River Marne, the Allied forces finally halted the Germans within 70 kilometres of Paris, thwarting the Schlieffen Plan. The Russians also mobilised faster than expected, and the Germans sent five divisions east to fight them. Knowing they no longer had the troop numbers or energy to encircle Paris—the men had been moving nonstop for a month—the Germans changed their plan and, instead, attacked the exposed left flank of the British and French forces.

DIGGING TO LIVE

In early September the French and British counterattacked, and drove the exhausted and overstretched Germans 64 kilometres back to the Aisne River, where they began digging trenches into the steep bank overlooking the river. After several unsuccessful attempts to take the bank, the British and French troops also dug in for protection. The first lines of the Western Front had been drawn.

The front-line lengthened as both sides tried and failed to get around each other's exposed flanks. Each time they were halted, the Germans dug trenches to avoid shells and bullets, and the British and French responded by digging their own trenches. In the 'race to the sea', the line lengthened northwards through France—through the Somme region and the towns of Arras and Armentières—and into Belgium, through Messines, and along the ridges overlooking Ypres in the Flanders region, until it reached the coastal town of Nieuport. The historic town of Ypres, just 50 kilometres from the coast, was one of the most vital areas of the front. If the Germans broke through there, they would have access to the English Channel.

On 20 October, four days after the New Zealanders had sailed from home, the Germans attacked the Belgian Army near Nieuport and the British on the strategic high ridges around Ypres. The Belgians eventually halted the German advance with French help, while the Germans and British continued to fight what became known as the First Battle of Ypres. The inexperienced German troops—some only 16 years old, many of them students—were no match for the professional British soldiers, who mowed them down in a day the Germans called the 'slaughter of the innocents'. But, as the Australians and New Zealanders steamed across the Indian Ocean towards Europe, the Germans forced the

TROOPSHIPS

The convoy of Australian and New Zealand troopships to Europe was escorted by three cruisers to guard it against enemy vessels. One German raider, SMS *Emden*—often mistaken for a British ship because of its fake fourth funnel—became the most hunted German ship in the war. It had sunk 15 merchant ships in September 1914 alone, as well as several naval vessels. En route, news reached the convoy that the SMS *Emden* was within three hours' sail. The Australian light cruiser HMAS *Sydney* steamed out to meet it, and after the two vessels had shelled each other for over an hour, the SMS *Emden* admitted defeat—it had been hit over 100 times. The survivors were transferred to the convoys, and many of the Australian and New Zealand troops took the opportunity to meet them.

British off Messines Ridge, and came as close as six kilometres to Ypres after vicious hand-to-hand battles on Menin Road. The name of Ypres was becoming infamous around the world.

THE LINES FORM

With winter approaching, and the front-lines now stretching 800 kilometres from the Swiss Alps to the Belgian coast, the generals on both sides ordered their men to consolidate their positions. The Germans dug trenches deep into the soil, or built sandbag walls on soggy ground. They situated them in areas easy to guard, often on the high ground overlooking the British and French. Every effort was put in to make the

New Zealander Corporal Gerald Sievers was in charge of guarding some of them and traded souvenirs with them, forming the opinion that they were 'good fellows'.

Two other German merchant raiders continued to cause headaches around New Zealand and Australia. One, commanded by Felix von Luckner, a young man who'd run away from home at the age of 13, captured the attention of the New Zealanders. In a three-masted sailing ship, Luckner was considered a pirate, boarding ships, taking prisoners and then sinking the vessels. Even when he was captured, he commandeered two boats in a failed escape attempt.

The SMS *Wolf*, a larger merchant raider, laid mines off the New Zealand and Australian coasts—some of which still wash up today. It captured numerous ships and returned to Germany filled with captured booty.

trenches defendable: the two-metre walls were riveted with wood, and wire was strung in front.

Villages, buildings, factories and cottages were incorporated into the lines. Cellars reinforced with concrete became dugouts, while concrete blockhouses constructed inside buildings held machine-gun nests with perfect fields of fire. The Germans had every reason to build up their trench systems: they had gained valuable land in Belgium and France, and now controlled much of France's iron supplies, which were essential for war.

Opposite them, across no-man's-land, the British and French also dug in; however, their trenches were not yet as advanced because they had no intention of just holding the line. Trenches were for defence and protection, whereas the Allies intended to advance and force the Germans from Belgium and France.

On 3 December, the Australians and New Zealanders landed at Alexandria, Egypt. Many were frustrated about not going straight to England and then the Western Front, but there wasn't enough accommodation for them. Britain also wanted extra troops in Egypt as defence against the Ottoman Empire—Turkey and parts of the Middle East—which had joined the war to side with Germany. In the desert, surrounded by pyramids, the men trained under the harsh sun and became known as the Anzacs—the Australian and New Zealand Army Corps.

At the Western Front, the soldiers battled the climate more than each other. On Christmas day, some German and British troops sang carols to each other, then climbed out into no-man's-land, where they shook hands. The truce lasted from several hours to days in some areas, with men sharing cigarettes and food and playing football. It would never happen again on that scale.

THE NEW YEAR DAWNS—1915

Despite enormous losses, the Great War was now a stalemate. The Germans maintained their defensive position on the Western Front and put their energy and resources into helping Austria defeat Russia on the Eastern Front, where a similar network of trenches had formed.

Russia had to survive; if it fell, the German commanders

would move all their troops to the Western Front, which would overwhelm the Allies. With fresh troops from Britain, Canada and India, major campaigns were launched along the Western Front to break the German lines and take pressure off the Russians by preventing the Germans from moving more troops to the Eastern Front. But the British and French couldn't break through.

Some British military commanders, like First Lord of the Admiralty Sir Winston Churchill, believed that the stalemate could be broken by knocking out those that supported Germany, in particular the Ottoman Empire, and a plan was made that would plunge the Anzacs into the war.

After a disastrous attempt by British battleships to sail up the Dardanelles Strait and capture the Ottoman capital, Constantinople (now called Istanbul), it was decided that Australian, New Zealand, French and British troops would land on the Gallipoli peninsula on 25 April 1915, cross overland and knock out the Turkish forts that had stopped the ships. It would be the Anzacs' first battle, and newspapers in both countries called it their 'Baptism of Fire'.

But the Turks halted the Anzacs on the hills overlooking the beaches. For eight months the Anzacs tried to break through. During this time news from the Western Front continued to reach the troops at Gallipoli. Three days before the Anzacs landed, the Germans had used poisonous gas for the first time in the Second Battle of Ypres. Carried on the wind, the green-yellow gas cloud killed thousands in minutes. The Germans had come within two kilometres of Ypres, but the town had still not fallen.

German submarines had also begun sinking any vessel approaching Britain, whether military or not. A British naval blockade was causing serious food shortages in Germany, and the Germans also wanted to starve Britain out of the war. But when one of their submarines sank the *Lusitania* passenger liner, killing more than 1100 people, the opinion of the world was further inflamed against them. The killing of Belgian civilians, the use of gas and now the sinking of the *Lusitania* were used as propaganda against the Germans. But the United States, with its large number of German-born citizens, remained neutral, though it warned Germany against sinking any further non-combat vessels.

In December, the battered, defeated Anzacs were evacuated from Gallipoli and returned to Egypt to guard against a possible Turkish invasion. Fresh Australian and New Zealand reinforcements, who'd continued to volunteer in their thousands, were already in Egypt, and, once they'd filled up the depleted battalions from Gallipoli, the remainder were used to create two new Australian divisions.

A FRESH START

Little had changed on the Western Front. Italy had sided with the British and French, but several Allied attempts to break through at Aubers Ridge and Loos had failed, despite longer artillery barrages of the German trenches and the British using gas for the first time. The failures resulted in

A German machine-gunner lying dead at his post, Somme region.
AWM E03351

Field Marshal French being replaced by General Sir Douglas Haig, who had led one of the British Army corps in the Battle of Mons. Haig, who'd served with the cavalry in the 1899–1902 Boer War, had been at the front since the beginning. He believed the outcome of the war would be decided at the Western Front, and that it would be won with a cavalry charge once the German troops had been worn down and a gap created in their line.

Both sides continued to look for ways to break the deadlock. The British, Russian, French and Italian commanders met at Chantilly in France on 6 December and agreed to fight with a common strategy—out of this, the British and French planned to attack the Germans at the Somme in July 1916. But the Germans struck first. Knowing it was no longer possible to break through to Paris, the new German commander, General Erich von Falkenhayn, set out to draw the French to one area—Verdun—and 'bleed' France 'to death'. Afterwards the smaller British force would have little choice but to surrender.

BLED WHITE—1916

Over several months the Germans concentrated over 1400 guns in the forests surrounding Verdun, in the north-east of France. Falkenhayn knew that the French would fight to the last man to hold the town, which was of great historic and symbolic importance.

On 21 February 1916, as the Anzacs continued training in the sliding sand of Egypt, the Germans struck at Verdun. The forts crumbled and trenches were churned to dust and blew away. As the French poured more troops into holding the town, the British ordered the Anzac corps to the Western Front. The newly formed I Anzac Corps—the 1st and 2nd Australian Divisions and the New Zealand Division—under Lieutenant General Sir William Birdwood, was to go first. The II Anzac Corps—the 4th and 5th Australian Divisions—under Lieutenant General Sir Alexander Godley, was to follow after more training.

KILLED IN ACTION

SERGEANT GERALD SIEVERS
Fell monger. 8 August 1915

PRIVATE LEONARD HURSE
Sheep farmer. 12 October 1917

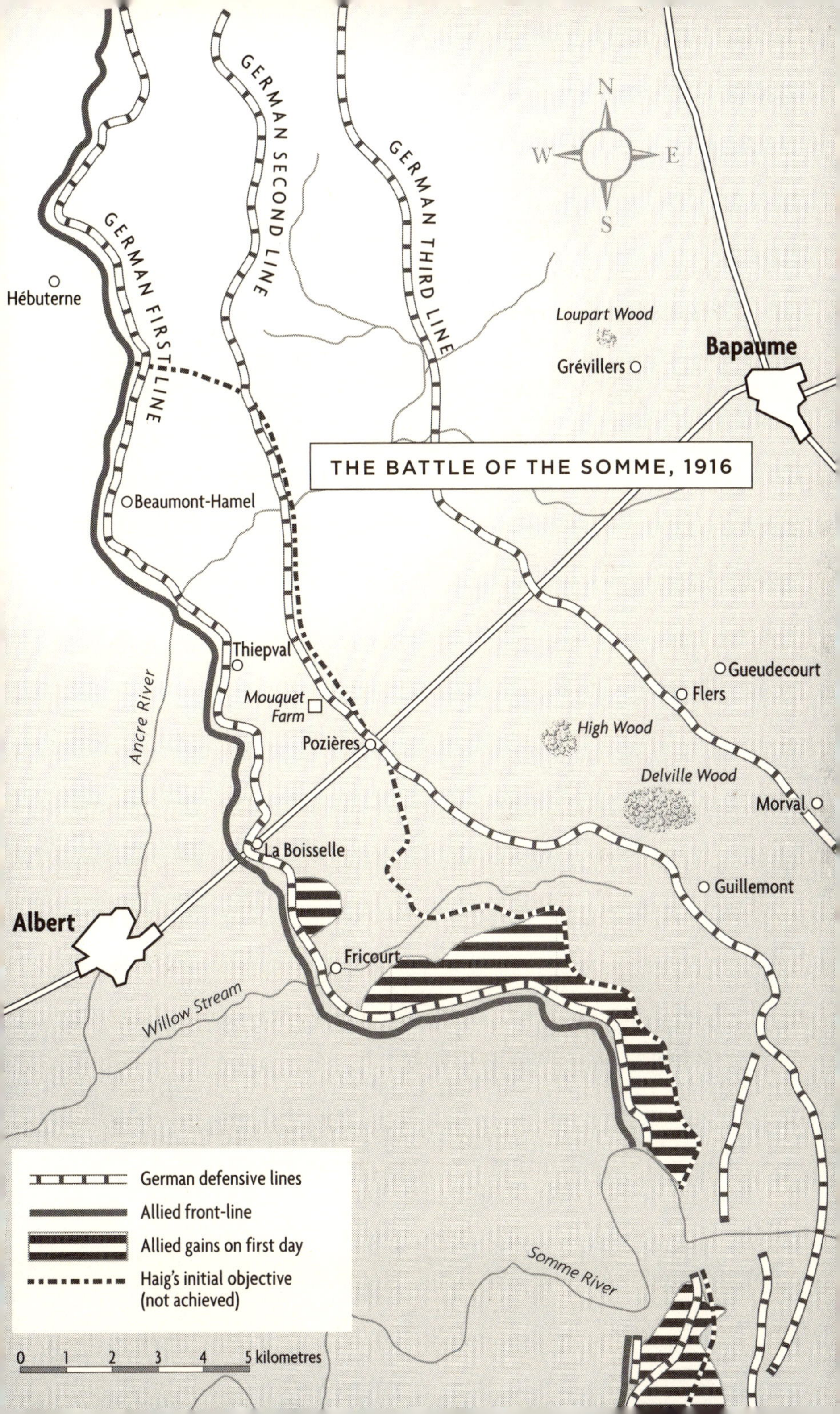
THE BATTLE OF THE SOMME, 1916
GERMAN FIRST LINE
GERMAN SECOND LINE
GERMAN THIRD LINE
N
W
E
S
Hébuterne
Loupart Wood
Grévillers
Bapaume
Beaumont-Hamel
Thiepval
Mouquet Farm
Pozières
Ancre River
Gueudecourt
Flers
High Wood
Delville Wood
Morval
La Boisselle
Guillemont
Albert
Fricourt
Willow Stream
Somme River
German defensive lines
Allied front-line
Allied gains on first day
Haig's initial objective (not achieved)
0 1 2 3 4 5 kilometres

CHAPTER TWO

RATHER LIKE HEAVEN, 1916

BLAKE—Killed in action on 19 July 1916 (previously reported missing). George Francis, No. 4737. late of 59th Bn, sailed only on March 7 of the same year.

I have lost my soul's companion
A life linked with my own
Each day I miss his footsteps
As I walk through life alone.

INSERTED BY HIS LOVING WIFE.

NEWSPAPER 'IN MEMORIAM' NOTICE

THE TRANSPORT SHIPS carrying I Anzac Corps from Egypt began reaching the southern French port of Marseilles on 19 March 1916. The soldiers were bound for Armentières, a British-held sector close to the Belgian border. The 58-hour train journey took the soldiers through lush green countryside being farmed by women, boys and old men. The men of fighting age were gone; they were dead, wounded or still fighting at the front, many at Verdun. The land was very different from what the Anzac corps had become used to in Egypt. 'It is an immense relief to be away from all the sand and dirt and smells,' wrote New Zealander Gunner Eric Burnett.

Just past Paris, the sky darkened and bitter winds lashed the slow-moving trains. Later, the troops disembarked and were billeted in villages several kilometres behind the front-line. Despite the distance, the soldiers could hear the dull rumble of artillery, particularly when the wind blew from the east. At night the horizon flickered with flares used to illuminate no-man's-land.

British soldiers and lorries crowded the countryside. The British, who held the front-line from Ypres in Belgium to the Somme River near Amiens in France, had over 1,263,000 troops in Europe, with 100,000 more arriving each month. They held 128 kilometres of trenches, while the French held 595 kilometres. Opposite them, 120 German divisions held the whole line. The British force was divided into four armies; the 40,000 Australians and 18,500 New Zealanders of I Anzac Corps were incorporated into General Sir Herbert Plumer's 2nd Army.

'THE BIG-LOOKED-FORWARD-TO DAY'

The Australians and New Zealanders were to take over a 16-kilometre sector from Armentières village to the Sugarloaf salient in front of the German-held village of Fromelles. It was a relatively quiet sector, nicknamed 'the Nursery', where newly arrived divisions were sent to gain experience. But before taking it over, the men trained—passing through gas-filled trenches wearing the cumbersome gasmasks, marching long distances on the cobbled roads and learning to lie down and not panic when faced with the gushing jet of the new German flamethrower. Even the grenades were different. Those who'd served at Gallipoli no longer needed to make their own from jam tins: they now had boxes of the new and more powerful Mills bombs.

After their training, the soldiers moved to villages closer to the front-line. Here the effects of war were more obvious: the guns were louder, and villages and farm buildings were either demolished or sandbagged for protection. They were used as billets, casualty clearing stations or army headquarters. Despite this, some farmers still worked their land, while school children ran about with gasmasks.

From 7 April, as German gun muzzles flickered in the distance, the Australian troops took over most of the 16-kilometre sector. The New Zealanders took charge of the rest on 13 May. Each of the three divisions was responsible for maintaining and protecting a small five- to six-kilometre zone. New Zealander Private Walter Carruthers, a Gallipoli veteran, felt 'quite happy now that we are into it again'. He was keen to see the Germans get 'a hiding', and hoped their army 'has to run like blazes and doesn't stop until he get across the Rhine'. Sergeant Cecil Malthus, another Gallipoli veteran from New Zealand, couldn't pretend to rejoice at going in again. 'The front line is rather like heaven,' he said, 'everybody writes it up but nobody really wants to go there.' Australian Sergeant James Makin called it 'the big-looked-forward-to day.' He was filled with questions:

> What will the actual trenches be like? What is the feeling of one 'under fire' for the first time? Are we to occupy a 'hot' part of the line, or a place of comparative quiet?

SANDBAGS, POPPIES AND WIRE

From their billets the soldiers walked down the cobbled streets, then slipped through hedges or broken walls into communication saps—protected lanes leading to the trenches. Here, the low-lying land was too wet to dig trenches and saps. Instead, 'breastworks'—12-metre-wide walls of sandbags—were constructed. The back areas were crowded with soldiers, ammunition dumps, war refuse, billets and hospitals, all within shelling range.

The breastworks, like the trenches, were not built in a straight line but zigzagged in a series of bays. They were in a bad way. The sandbags were mildewy and sprouting grass, while the duckboards—wooden boards laid over muddy ground—rotted under stagnant water. Barbed-wire barriers protected the breastworks of both sides and between them was a no-man's-land of damaged trees, long grass, crimson poppies and self-sown crops. In places no-man's-land was as narrow as 55 metres, in others it stretched to 270 metres wide.

The land sloped slightly up to the German lines, where snipers and machine-gunners watched for anyone who showed themselves above the sandbags. The snipers fired through concealed loopholes in the sandbag parapet, or from trees. The machine guns were concealed behind steel screens and sandbags. The strategic placement of these guns prevented enemy soldiers charging across no-man's-land without proper planning. Fortunately, the German artillery wasn't as active here as in other sectors, but this meant the Australians and New Zealanders weren't as careful as they needed to be. Aeroplanes—made of wood and canvas—were still a novelty in 1916 and the men stood out in the open to watch them dogfighting, or dodging anti-aircraft fire. At first they had been used only for observation but now they carried machine guns. Air dominance was essential for obtaining information about enemy trenches and movement. Observers also spied from church towers, trees or the baskets of gas-filled balloons.

On 19 April, Australian troops were spotted lighting fires and hanging out clothes around their billets three kilometres behind the front-line. Within a few minutes, German shells had killed or wounded over 70 and destroyed the farm building. The Australians and New Zealanders quickly learned to be as inconspicuous as the Germans opposite them.

A NUMBING FURY

Shortly after the Australians arrived, a German morse code message flashed:

'Australians go home.'

'Why?' the Australians signalled back.

'We are too good,' was the answer.

The Nursery became more deadly as the joint Somme offensive planned by the British and French at Chantilly drew near. To distract the Germans from the military build-up at the Somme, 100 kilometres south of Armentières, the artillery in other sectors increased its shelling of the enemy line. The Germans retaliated and their exploding shells heaved and shook the ground like earthquakes. The high-explosive shells tore holes in the breastworks and ripped men in half. Many were killed by the concussion waves alone. New Zealander Rifleman William Wilson was stunned after German shells exploded nearby:

> [For] about six seconds after the explosion, you don't know if anything is wrong or not. It sort of numbs you. The hot stifling gases mixed with dust and black smoke choke you. You can't see for falling earth and clay and your ears ring like fury.

Hour after hour, the shells shrieked down and the men tensed as they waited for them to hit. They started differentiating between them by the noise they made or other telltale signs—the 'rum-jar' mortar left a trail of sparks as it turned end over end through the air. Guessing where they were likely to land, the men dove for cover in other bays.

But when the shells came over thick and fast, they could do nothing but claw into the ground.

They gave the shells nicknames like Jack Johnson, Coal Box, Silent Susan and Whizz-Bang. Close-firing mortars that could be launched from the trenches were also nicknamed—Rum Jar, Toffee Apple, Flying Pig and Plum Pudding. Most shells were named for their shape or sound, but the Jack Johnson was named after the 1908 world heavyweight boxing champion.

The artillery had quickly become the decisive weapon of the war, used to smother trenches before attacks or to bombard no-man's-land if troops in the front-line fired SOS signal rockets to indicate that enemy troops were crossing. The rockets burst in different colours and sequences to inform commanders further back about what was happening at the front. Certain rockets signalled that a sector was being attacked, while different colours signalled the end of an action or indicated new positions. In the lead-up to major battles, and during them, each side's artillery tried to silence the other, which would give its own infantry a marked advantage.

DEADLY NIGHTS

On 5 May, two weeks after the morse code message, German shells plunged into the Australian trenches. The roar of the hurricane bombardment was deafening. In the light of the shell bursts, several groups of Germans, with daggers, revolvers and bombs, were spotted bursting into the Australian trenches. They shot anyone who showed resistance, bombed dugouts and killed men by cracking their heads with knobkerries—wooden shafts with metal studs at the ends. Twenty-five minutes later, they were gone, taking 11 prisoners and leaving 95 dead or wounded. Soon after, the Australians began preparing their own raids.

With preparations for the Somme offensive intensifying, General Haig—the British commander—had ordered an increase in raids to prevent the Germans from thinning their trenches and moving spare troops to the area. Raiders trained at night using replicas of the German trenches created from information gathered by spotter aeroplanes. On their allotted night, they blackened their faces and hands, painted their bayonets, and swapped rifles for revolvers and knobkerries. With a curtain of explosives protecting them and illuminating the trenches in flashes, the raiders—some wearing steel body armour—stormed through the German trenches, bombed dugouts and captured prisoners. Any German who didn't cooperate was killed, but the men also shot some who'd surrendered—they had orders to take only a certain number of prisoners. Then, on a signal, the raiding parties withdrew. They were in and out like a whirlwind, sometimes in as little as eight minutes.

Not all raids succeeded. The Germans bombed one New Zealand group spotted sneaking through a gap in the wire. In another raid, a wounded Australian soldier was left behind. The Germans put up a sign saying he was being cared for 'and is hopful'. Earlier, the Germans had used a placard to inform the New Zealanders that the German Navy had defeated the British in the Battle of Jutland. The Australians shelled the placard, while the New Zealanders replied with their own sign, stating how many German ships had been sunk.

THE SOMME

The German positions at the Somme were formidable. Trenches had been dug into the chalk, and the shell-ruined villages and forests had been fortified with deep wire entanglements and concrete strong points, strategically placed to give each German machine-gun position covering fire. The first and second German trench systems ran along ridges overlooking the British, while the third system, several kilometres back, was still being constructed.

The Somme had been chosen because it was where the British and French lines joined. Initially the French were to take the lead role, but, with the Battle of Verdun drawing away many of their divisions, the British took over. Despite having fewer divisions and the attacking line being reduced to 33 kilometres, Haig expected his troops to break the first German trench system within three hours, and the second by the third day. Then the cavalry would gallop through the break and circle in behind the German lines. If this failed, the commanders simply wanted more Germans killed than their own men. At the very least they hoped to take pressure off the French at Verdun.

The British massed the largest number of guns used in one offensive to date—over 1400—and opened fire on

25 June. On one day alone over 200,000 shells were fired. For seven days, the British bombarded the German lines. The explosions were so loud they could be heard in London, but many of the shells were duds and too many were filled with shrapnel balls, designed to explode in the air and kill troops. They did not damage the dugouts the Germans were sheltering in. Nor did they destroy the barbed wire as the commanders believed they would.

At 7.30 a.m. on 1 July, British officers blew their whistles and bugles, and the soldiers climbed out of their trenches and formed long, evenly spaced lines, then marched forward. Just before they charged, the four platoons of Captain Wilfred Percy Nevill's company each kicked a football to see who could get it furthest across no-man's-land, in places 640 metres wide.

The German troops hauled up their machine guns and mowed the enemy down; many British soldiers were hit as they left their trenches. The long front and the lack of reliable communication caused confusion. British troops reached several villages and some sections of the first German line. But the majority had been stopped. By the end of the day, there were 60,000 British casualties—20,000 had died, most within the first hour.

TOO LITTLE GAINED

Over the next two weeks, as the next phase was planned, the British launched 46 localised and uncoordinated attacks in which they gained 52 square kilometres of ground, but they still hadn't broken through the first line. Then, on 14 July, after an intense artillery bombardment, 22,000 British soldiers took the Germans by surprise, sweeping through their first line and capturing 10 kilometres of their second line before they recovered. The day was a huge success; the troops had broken the lines, although fighting continued among the dense trees of Delville and High woods.

The Somme offensive forced the Germans to end their assault against Verdun—where over 140,000 Germans and 180,000 French had been killed or wounded—and it was now the hot spot of the war. To prevent the British breaking through, the Germans began directing fresh troops to the Somme from quieter areas, like Armentières. Wanting to stop the Germans further thinning their trenches, Haig ordered that the raids continue.

Several weeks earlier, Lieutenant General Godley had arrived from Egypt with the 4th and 5th Australian Divisions of II Anzac Corps. Now there were over 100,000 Australian and New Zealand troops at the Western Front. After a reshuffle of divisions, I Anzac Corps consisted of the 1st, 2nd and 4th Australian Divisions, while II Anzac Corps had the New Zealand Division and the 5th Division. The I Anzac Corps was moved down to Messines, 10 kilometres away, while the New Zealanders undertook the raids at Armentières. But the raids were failing, and a more threatening action was needed to hold the German troops in the area.

Lieutenant General Sir Richard Haking, a British divisional commander stationed beside the 5th Australian

Division, wanted to capture the part of the German front-line known as the Sugarloaf salient, near the occupied village of Fromelles on Aubers Ridge, 12 kilometres south of Armentières. The Sugarloaf, which was choked with machine guns and concrete bunkers, bulged into the British line in low-lying farmland overgrown with grass and weeds. Haking had already been involved in two attacks against Aubers Ridge, in May 1915 and June 1916. Both had failed against the strong German defences. But Haig agreed to Haking's plan, and Godley lent Haking the newly arrived 5th Division.

A POINTLESS TRICK

Haking's plan was that the 5th Division, with the weakened 61st British Division on their right, would advance in waves to capture the German front-line and the support trenches beyond it. Shortly before the attack, one of Haig's staff suggested it be cancelled: there wasn't enough ammunition for the artillery, and the flat 360-metre expanse of no-man's-land—the length of three rugby fields—was too wide to cross successfully. Haking insisted the attack go ahead. The troops, he said, were 'worked up' to do it, and any change 'would have a bad effect' on them. The commander of the 5th Division, Major General Sir James McCay, kept quiet. He was happy enough that his division, the last to arrive in France, would be the first to take part in a serious action, despite half the men not having seen the front-line, let alone fought in a battle.

In the German breastworks, with their concrete machine-gun shelters, and from Fromelles village one and a half kilometres back, German observers had watched the British and Australian preparations. They put up a sign saying 'Advance Australia. If you can!'

Late in the morning of 19 July, as the Australians passed British graves from 1915 on their way to the front-line, over 320 guns opened fire on the German trenches. Some of the troops still wore their slouch hats because there weren't enough helmets to go around. It was a hot day. The Australians cheered as the shells tore ragged gaps in the German breastworks and heaved them into the air.

But the German troops, including 28-year-old Lance Corporal Adolf Hitler, hunkered down in their concrete dugouts, listening to the replying bark of their artillery. For hours their shells destroyed the Australian trenches. Men hugged the parapets to avoid shrapnel, standing on the dead, as stretcher-bearers laboured to remove the wounded. One soldier, driven mad by the constant shelling, kept calling for his mum to close the gate. An officer cried like a child; other men just babbled.

MORE HOPELESS

With another 15 minutes of the Allied bombardment left, the Australians moved out into no-man's-land. The 8th Brigade was on the far left, the 14th Brigade was in the middle and the 15th Brigade was on the right, directly opposite the Sugarloaf and with the furthest to go. The 61st British Division was attacking next to the 15th. Despite dust and smoke smothering the land and making it difficult to see, the 15th Brigade commander, Brigadier General Harold 'Pompey' Elliot, was confident the artillery had done its job. He told his men, 'You won't find a German in the trenches when you get there.' When zero hour arrived, at 6 p.m., the 15th Brigade charged through an overgrown orchard and across a shallow river. The Germans at the Sugarloaf hauled out their machine guns and waited in the low summer sun until they had a clear view, then started firing. Their bullets ripped into trees and sparked off the wire. The attacking troops dove into shell holes or the river. When men of the following waves 'looked over the top, they saw no-man's-land leaping up everywhere in showers of dust and sand'. They also saw men hit with so many bullets that their bodies were cut in two. Still, at five-minute intervals, the waves of men charged. For Sergeant Walter Downing, it was like the charge of the Light Horse at Gallipoli, 'but more terrible, more hopeless'.

No-man's-land on the left of the Sugarloaf was narrower, and the 8th and 14th Brigades swept across it and into the enemy trench before the Germans had time to react. After bayoneting and shooting anyone in their path, the Australians moved on to capture the support trenches, but all they could find were open grassy fields crossed with hedges and a watery ditch filled with corpses 180 metres beyond the German front-line. The ditch had at one point been the Germans' support line but it was now flooded and abandoned. At 6.30 p.m., unaware that the 15th Brigade and the British to their right had been shot to pieces and that the

Sugarloaf wasn't captured, one of the battalion commanders, Lieutenant Colonel Frederick Toll, scrawled a note saying his men were digging in. He attached it to a messenger pigeon, the safest and most reliable means of communication available. The bird took 17 minutes to fly the several kilometres back to headquarters. By the time the message was read and fresh orders given, events at the front were changing.

A BUTCHER'S SHOP

Toll returned to the unoccupied German front-line with most of his men, leaving some of his troops from the 8th and 14th Brigades to make the 45-centimetre-deep, 900-metre-long watery 'support line' ditch defendable. The men scraped the clay mud off their entrenching tools into the two empty sandbags they each carried, hopelessly trying to build a wall. Ammunition and sandbags were running low, but the carrying parties bringing up supplies were being shot down. Meanwhile, engineers raced to dig communications saps between the Allied line and the captured German front-line. The shallow river in no-man's-land was bloated with 'wounded and dying men—like a butcher's shop—men groaning and crying and shrieking'. When the carriers did reach the front, many stayed to fight rather than returning for more supplies.

With messages arriving that the men were digging in, the Australian commanders believed there was still every chance of success, even though the 15th Brigade and the British hadn't reached the Sugarloaf. A new attack to begin at

9 p.m. was planned to capture it, but at the last moment Haking ordered the British troops to wait until the morning. The Australian staff were told, but the message wasn't passed on to Elliot until half of his reserve battalion had already advanced into the dwindling light. Out in no-man's-land, soldiers from the earlier waves rose from craters to join the charge, but machine-gunners on the Sugarloaf shot them down.

A LONG BLURRY NIGHT

With only the 8th and 14th Brigades now fighting, German reinforcements moved out of a ruined farm, known as 'Dead Sow Farm', to attack the isolated soldiers in the ditch. Men from the 8th Brigade were closest to the farm and took the brunt of the attack. But the Germans were quickly shot down by machine guns that the Australians had moved forward. Shelling had blocked the river's flow and the water was rising in the ditch. Unless the wounded were spotted and pulled out in time, they drowned. When the men's rifles became clogged with mud, they took dry ones from the dead. Behind them, in the captured front-line, Toll and his men worked to make the middle section secure, building up the destroyed breastworks with rotten, disintegrating sandbags and German corpses.

Then the Germans rushed down from the uncaptured Sugarloaf and moved along the empty zigzagging breastworks of their old front-line from the right, towards Toll. As they did they drew parallel with the men of the 14th Brigade in the ditch. Flares of white stars lit up a night 'blurred by dust and smoke' and the 14th Brigade could see the spikes of German helmets moving behind them. Realising they were about to be cut off from the captured German front-line and consequently their own lines, a group charged the Germans across the open ground. They were shot down, and the survivors were forced to scramble back to the ditch.

The Germans kept moving down their old front-line towards the middle section and Toll. Bombers were sent to stop them getting further behind the men in the ditch, and when the bombers and Germans met, as many as 12 bombs were 'in the air at a time'. Slowly, the Germans were pushed back towards the Sugarloaf. Then, at 3.15 a.m., Germans from Dead Sow Farm attacked the 8th Brigade again, overrunning part of the ditch, and reoccupying the left section of their old front-line.

The Australians had been fighting for nine hours. With Germans now back on both sides of their old line and still moving out of Dead Sow Farm, the exhausted men in the ditch were faced with a choice of surrendering or dying. Over 150 of the 8th Brigade charged back, pouring into the reoccupied German trench, where they fought savagely with the enemy, before scrambling out and rushing back towards their own trenches. Two men out of a group of 11 who'd made a pact to stick together were caught in the trench. The other nine returned to help them, then they rushed across no-man's-land. All but one made it. He was shot dead as they reached the wire entanglements.

With news reaching McCay and Haking that the 8th Brigade had retreated and the Germans were back in either end of their original front-line, Haking ordered the last Australians to withdraw. As the sky grew lighter, Toll's men in the German front-line streamed down the communication trench back to the Australian line. Those still in the ditch had no escape; the Germans were behind them. Some surrendered; others kept fighting—calling desperately for reinforcements. When they ran out of ammunition they reached for their bayonets but by 9 a.m. the attempt to capture the Sugarloaf was over. In one bombing post, seven men lay motionless in the mud.

CRYING OUT

For three more hours the German artillery pounded the smashed Australian trenches, which were filled with the dead and dying, blood and mud caking their uniforms. At midday, the shelling stopped. The ensuing stillness was broken only by the cries of the wounded lying in no-man's-land. The 'wounded could be seen everywhere raising their limbs in pain or turning hopelessly, hour after hour, from one side to the other.' They called for help and for water as the sun burned them and flies crawled over their faces and their wounds. German bullets smacked into any that tried to crawl back. In the trenches, men sat in a state of shock, staring at nothing.

Later, while some men ate cold bully beef from the tin, others slipped out into no-man's-land, taking advantage of

Australian dead lying in a gap in a barbed-wire entanglement, Somme region. AWM E03149

an informal offer by a German officer to let the wounded be collected. But when McCay found out, he ended the truce—no informal negotiations were allowed with the Germans.

The Australians then risked their lives on mercy missions. Three hundred men were brought back on the first night, but the following day no-man's-land was still cluttered with men. One soldier with a serious head wound walked around in circles, collapsed then got up and walked again. No one could reach him. He kept walking, collapsing, getting up, until a German sniper shot him, perhaps to end his misery. The Australians drew lots to decide who would venture into no-man's-land for the wounded. Sergeant Major Arthur Brunton wrote a farewell to his wife, 'perhaps for the last time, though I hope not'. Second Lieutenant Simon Fraser, a Victorian farmer, was bringing back a wounded soldier when someone else called out, 'Don't forget me, cobber.' When Fraser returned with reinforcements to collect the wounded man, another soldier screamed, 'Stretcher-bearer! stretcher-bearer!' then 'Come on New South Wales.' He'd been out there for three days, and when he was finally brought in, his wound was fly-blown.

Many others weren't found, and they died in no-man's-land. Private Algernon Bell wrote in his diary that he was wounded 'in arm and leg. Going to try and crawl back to trenches tonight'. He made it, but died four days later.

The first battle that the Australians fought on the Western Front was a complete failure. Over 5500 had been killed or wounded and 400 taken prisoner. In one day, the Australians suffered one-fifth of the casualties sustained during their eight months at Gallipoli. As his men returned, Elliot cried. In the 60th Battalion alone, only one officer and 106 men out of 887 made it to the morning roll call. Almost nothing had been gained. And the Germans had been distracted from the Somme for just a moment.

In his report, Haking said that the artillery barrage was strong and that the attack had failed because the British lacked fighting spirit and the Australians 'were not sufficiently trained to consolidate the ground gained'. This ignored the fact that the ultimate objective—the German support lines—had turned out to be water-filled ditches. They 'lost heavily', he wrote, but he felt that, despite the failure, the battle had done both the Australian and the British division 'a great deal of good'.

The British headquarters dressed up the failure as a successful raid. In Australia, the newspapers followed the British communiqué:

> Yesterday evening, south of Armentières, we carried out some important raids on a front of two miles in which Australian troops took part. About 140 German prisoners were captured.

In reality, the 5th Division had been wiped out and the survivors were demoralised. They were learning what war on the Western Front was like. Lieutenant Ronald McInnis wrote that 'We thought we knew something of the horrors of war but we were mere recruits and have had our full education in one day.' The men of I Anzac Corps were about to find out for themselves. As the Germans buried the Australian dead in mass graves, the three divisions of the corps—the 1st, 2nd and 4th Australian Divisions—moved from Messines down to the Somme.

KILLED IN ACTION

LANCE CORPORAL GEORGE BLAKE
Carpenter. 19 July 1916

SECOND LIEUTENANT WALTER CARRUTHERS
Bank clerk. 29 September 1918

DIED OF WOUNDS

PRIVATE ALGERNON BELL
Fireman. 24 July 1916

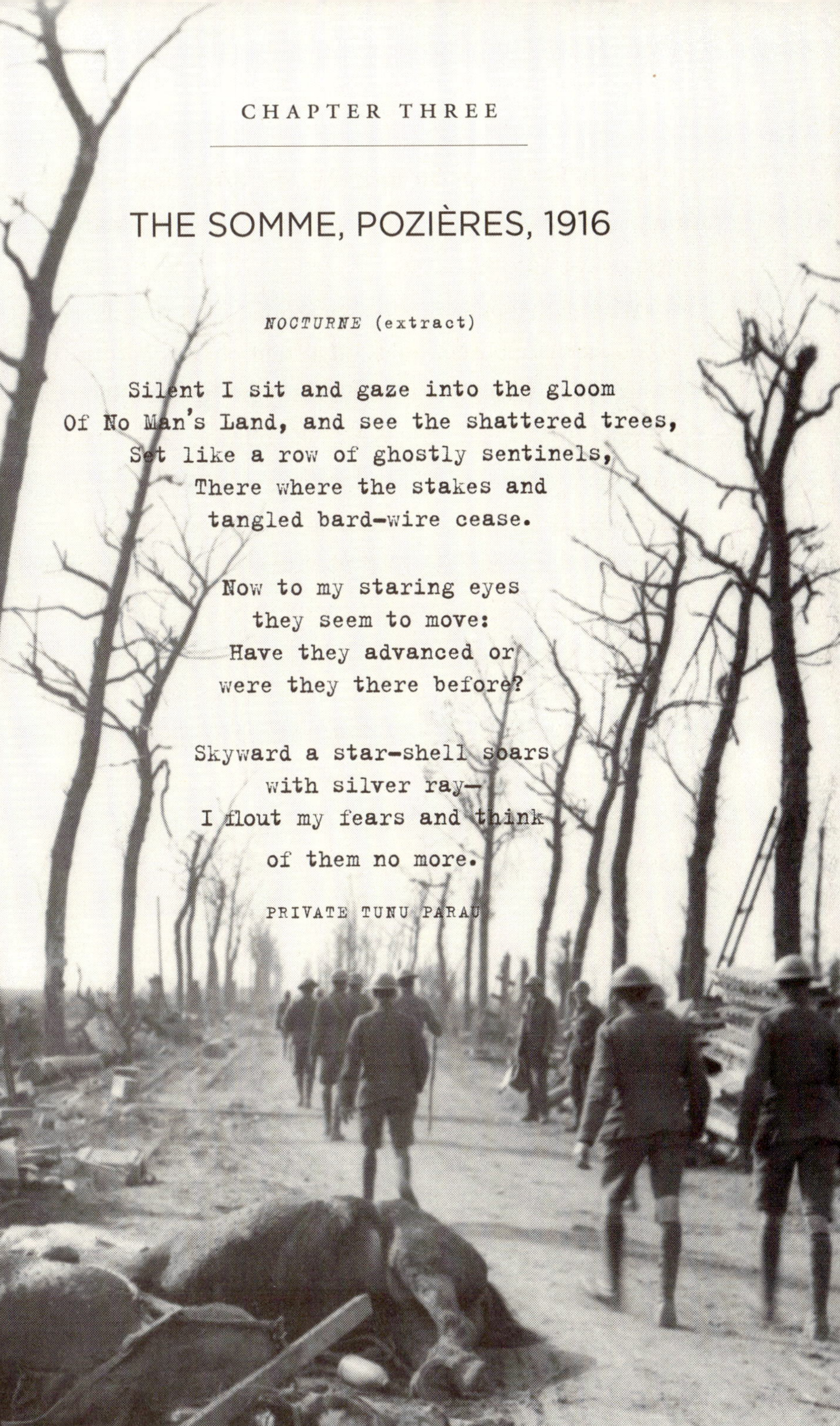

CHAPTER THREE

THE SOMME, POZIÈRES, 1916

NOCTURNE (extract)

Silent I sit and gaze into the gloom
Of No Man's Land, and see the shattered trees,
Set like a row of ghostly sentinels,
There where the stakes and
tangled bard-wire cease.

Now to my staring eyes
they seem to move:
Have they advanced or
were they there before?

Skyward a star-shell soars
with silver ray—
I flout my fears and think
of them no more.

PRIVATE TUNU PARAU

IN THE HOT sun on 20 July, the 1st Australian Division waited in a hastily dug trench that faced the tree-lined streets of the German-occupied hamlet of Pozières and the two formidable trenches of the second German line (known as Old German Lines) on a ridge 450 metres behind it. Whoever held Pozières had control of the highest point of the battlefield. General Sir Henry Rawlinson considered it the key to the area, and General Haig wanted it captured. British troops had tried to take the hamlet on the first day of the Somme offensive, nearly three weeks earlier. But the Germans had held on through that attack and four others, and the bodies of British dead hung in the wire.

On 19 July, the men of the 1st Division had left their billets and marched 15 kilometres, leaving behind the green countryside as they got closer to the front-line. Just before the town of Albert, the men put on their tin hats, and officers discarded their 'Sam Browne' revolver belts so snipers couldn't easily distinguish their rank. They passed under a golden statue of the Virgin Mary and child hanging from a shelled cathedral in Albert. The Australians nicknamed her 'Fanny Durack' after the 1912 Olympic swimming and diving champion. The statue was by now famous and symbolic—both sides believed its fall would signify the end of the war. Then the Australians crossed a shell-holed land and barely recognisable German trenches. In the dark, they moved through a gas attack into the trench facing Pozières—the gas smelled sweet, like hyacinths.

The I Anzac Corps was now under the command of

General Sir Hubert Gough of the Reserve Army (soon to become the 5th Army), a relatively inexperienced British general who wanted immediate results. On 18 July, Gough had told the 1st Division commander, Lieutenant General Sir Harold Walker, 'I want you to go into the line and attack Pozières tomorrow night.' Walker, feeling that he might be rushed into an action that was 'hasty or ill-considered' argued for a postponement. The date was set for 23 July, when Haig's third great effort on the Somme would begin. Six divisions, stretched from Pozières to Guillemont, would advance—the Australians were to attack Pozières; the British, Guillemont. After proper artillery preparations, the Australians were to overrun Pozières trench, which surrounded the hamlet, and go on to capture a main road running through its centre.

HAIL STORM

As zero hour approached, the men's fears grew. It was the worst time, the waiting. According to Lieutenant Ben Champion, 'The tension affected the men in different ways. I couldn't stop urinating, and we were all anxious for the barrage to begin.' Men re-read letters, looked at photos they carried in their breast pocket, wrote farewell letters, prayed silently or chain-smoked to calm their nerves. Some vomited; others told jokes. No one wanted to let themselves or their comrades down.

Three hours after sunset on 22 July, the first waves went 'over the bags' and, keeping low, moved up close to the enemy line, where they waited for zero hour. The Germans waited inside their dugouts; one soldier wrote to his wife and children that he was in 'Hell's trenches', and had 'given up hope of life' and would think of them to his last moment. Then the artillery struck. German flares floated downwards as the British bombarded them with such intensity that the shell bursts could be seen 30 kilometres away. The gunners loaded and fired shells as fast as they could. This was the bombardment the Australians had needed at Fromelles.

At 12.30 a.m., as the artillery lifted off Pozières trench and back to the orchards on the hamlet's outskirts, officers blew their whistles and the first wave charged. They quickly overcame the shell-shocked Germans holding Pozières trench. Following waves passed over the trench, stumbling over shell holes, through dark hedges and the remains of gardens and houses, to reach what was left of the main street. A three-metre-high reinforced concrete blockhouse was the only structure still standing; out of a slit poked a machine-gun muzzle. The Australians charged from the side, surprising the 25 Germans inside. Down in the lower chamber, Private Jack Bourke found parcels and several letters addressed to soldiers in children's handwriting. Nearby was a German trench coat with a blood-stained shrapnel hole.

The Australians gained the only notable success that day; the British troops had failed to secure Guillemont.

During the day, the Australians shot down three German attempts to recapture the hamlet, then rested or searched the nearby ruins, dugouts and German dead for souvenirs. As they waited for night, the two colonels in charge of the next advance received an 'urgent and secret' message that insisted the Australians had to be more disciplined and must salute all British officers, even those driving past in cars. That night the 1st Division captured the rest of Pozières, but from seven o'clock the next morning, the German artillery responded, and for the next three days their shells fell like hail. At times, 15 to 20 shells a minute were bursting in the same spot. The Germans had abandoned the idea of recapturing Pozières, so their gunners set out to make it unliveable. Trenches disappeared and the debris from one exploding shell would simply fill in the crater next to it. Men were blown to pieces, or killed by the concussion waves from the blasts. Others were buried alive. If they were lucky, their comrades dug them out in time and they gasped for breath as the air about them shrieked and whistled with incoming shells. On 25 July, Sergeant Leonard Elvin wrote:

> Heavy firing all morning—simply murder. Men falling everywhere...expecting death every second. 23 men smothered in one trench. Dead and dying everywhere. Some simply blown to pieces.

Many men couldn't cope. One runner, unable to face the barrage again, handed over his last message and shot himself. Others delivered their messages then fell dead from wounds.

With the shelling making it difficult to remove the wounded, Private Edward Jenkins, a bushman from New South Wales, worked with others to carry as many as they could to safer areas. Jenkins set up shelters for them and gave out the last of his water. His officers considered him a larrikin and a troublemaker, but at Pozières he worked tirelessly and without orders until a shell killed him as he was carrying his dixie of tea to give to the wounded.

The bombardment was as severe as any experienced at the Somme or Verdun, and when it died down, on 26 July, over 5000 Australians had been killed or wounded in their seven days in the front-line. When the 1st Division was relieved by the 2nd Australian Division during the night of 27 July, the men marched out, dazed and staring into space, some wearing souvenired German spike helmets and belts inscribed with the motto '*Gott mit uns*'—God with us.

POZIÈRES HEIGHTS

The 2nd Division was confronted with a land littered with blackened, bloated, fly-ridden bodies and limbs. German shells continued to pulverise Pozières to dust and ash. With the trenches levelled, supply parties had to walk over tracks in the open. There was no safe place to rest. Men expected death or to be buried, 'dug out and buried again'. One group tried to distract themselves by playing cards. When their sergeant was killed, they threw his body out of the trench, then kept playing until an exploding shell killed them all.

Even though the Germans were clearly expecting an attack, General Gough insisted that the Australians seize the Old German Lines on the heights behind Pozières. The 2nd Division commander, Major General Gordon Legge, did not ask for a postponement despite a report from an artillery commander that the dust and haze meant he couldn't be certain that the wire had been cut. Legge, commanding a battle of this scale for the first time, was certain that the entanglements would be cut in time. Just after midnight on 29 July, the Australians advanced. It took them eight long minutes to cross no-man's-land, and, as flares turned night to day, the German machine guns opened fire. The bombardment hadn't pierced the wire and the men that made it through the gunfire used wire-cutters, their rifle butts and their bare hands to try to get through. Men fell dead or wounded into the wire, which tightened around the living as they struggled.

In half an hour, 2000 men had been killed or wounded. As the 2nd Division withdrew, the sky was lit with red and green German flares of success. General Haig reminded the Australian commanders that they weren't fighting Turks any more but the 'most scientific and most military nation in Europe'. Legge insisted his men be given another go, but this time the attack would begin only when everything was properly prepared—a one-metre-deep jumping-off trench would be dug closer to the German trenches.

DOING IT PROPERLY

On the night of 31 July, 500 soldiers moved into no-man's-land to dig the trench. Melbourne journalist Lieutenant John Raws, unaware that his brother had been killed in the previous attack and was lying in no-man's-land, reached the jumping-off point to find soldiers and officers alike losing their nerve through the constant shelling. After one officer was killed and, according to Raws, 'the strain had sent two other officers mad', Raws and a fellow officer took over and insisted that the digging be finished. The dead and wounded were no longer to be buried or carried out. The soldiers' only task was to dig. Another officer, driven to the edge, ordered the men to retire, but Raws threatened to shoot anyone who left.

For five nights, the men dug the jumping-off line under shellfire. Some fled into the dark to escape the noise and fear. Raws wrote:

> I have had much luck and kept my nerve so far. The awful difficulty is to keep it. The bravest of all often lose it—courage does not count here. It is all nerve—once that goes one becomes a gibbering maniac…
>
> And forests! There are not even tree trunks left, not a leaf or a twig. All is buried, and churned up again, and buried again. The sad part is that one can see no end of this. If we live to-night, we have to go through to-morrow night, and next week, and next month. Poor wounded devils you meet on the stretchers are laughing with glee. One cannot blame them—they are getting out of this…
>
> …We are lousy, stinking, ragged, unshaven, sleepless…I have one puttee, a dead man's helmet, another dead man's gas protector, a dead man's bayonet. My tunic is rotten with other men's blood, and partly spattered with a comrade's brains.

As Raws left, he and three others helped a wounded man, using Raws' puttee to tie the man's severed leg to his pack.

On 4 August, the 2nd Division lay in the newly completed jumping-off line. The moment their artillery shells stopped hitting the German trenches, they rushed across the shortened no-man's-land and quickly captured the two almost flattened trenches of the Old German Lines on the ridge behind Pozières. In the 10 days that the 2nd Division had been in the line, 6800 had been killed or wounded.

A GERMAN REPLY

With only two days' experience in trenches at Armentières, on 6 August the 4th Australian Division relieved the 2nd Division. Several attempts to recapture the heights had already been shot down, but the Germans were determined. General Falkenhayn, the German commander, had insisted from the start of the war that no land was to be relinquished without a fight and that lost land was to be recaptured at the first opportunity. But with German commanders rushing counter-attacks, the Germans were now being as mauled as the Allies.

At dawn on 7 August, as the 4th Division sheltered in captured dugouts from a systematic bombardment, the Germans attacked again. The heights were lightly held by the Australians to prevent loss of life during heavy shelling, and three battalions of German troops swept over the battered trenches, stopping only to roll bombs into the dugouts and to leave sentries at the exits before the rest moved down the slope towards Pozières.

In one dugout, Lieutenant Albert Jacka, who had won a Victoria Cross for his actions at Gallipoli, fired his revolver up the stairs over two wounded soldiers, killing the German stationed at the top. Jacka and seven others prepared to dash back through the Germans to Pozières, but when they saw 40 Australian prisoners under a guard of the same number being led back towards the new German lines, Jacka lined up his men and charged.

The German guards opened fire, hitting every man—Jacka was hit seven times—but they reached the guards and a savage bayonet and fist-fight erupted, with the prisoners also attacking their guards. More raced over to join in, until

> Huns and Aussies were scattered in ones and twos all along the side of the hill...Each Aussie seemed as if he was having a war all on his own.

The Germans, now outnumbered, surrendered. When Jacka was carried out, few gave him any chance of survival, but he recovered and returned to the Western Front, serving until he was poisoned by gas in 1918.

A GRINDING ADVANCE—8 AUGUST TO 5 SEPTEMBER

With Pozières heights now secured, General Haig ordered the commanders in the area to organise their own attacks while he built up new divisions and ammunition for a September advance. Under General Gough, the Australians were to advance towards Mouquet Farm—a German strong point—to get in behind Thiepval, another bastion of the

German line. Over the next 28 days, the 1st, 2nd and 4th Australian Divisions were all used as Gough ordered attack after attack to drive a narrow salient two kilometres to the farm. The Germans made them fight for every metre, shelling their salient from the front and both sides. Fresh battalions were sent to the front via different routes to prevent them seeing the dead bodies from the previous attacks. When the ground was 'spongy' underfoot, the men realised they were stepping on corpses.

Twenty-year-old Sergeant David Badger wrote to his parents in South Australia, saying:

> When you see this I'll be dead; don't worry...Try to think I did the only possible thing, as I tell you I would do it again if I had the chance.

He died in the next attack.

The Australians hated the shallow advances on narrow fronts—now reduced to one or two battalions—and many felt they were just being sent to kill Germans. In one Australian's opinion, 'All we are doing is using up German Reserves, and, at a faster rate, our own.' Even the New Zealand commander, Major General Sir Andrew Russell, believed the Australians were being wasted.

The tactics created bitterness towards the commanders, and a feeling that no one knew what they, the soldiers, were going through. In their view, the newspapers reported only the official line about successful attacks, with no mention of the human cost. Corporal Arthur Thomas wrote that a 'book on the life of an infantryman' needed to be written to 'quickly prevent these shocking tragedies'. Captain Gordon Maxfield felt that

> Nothing published in the papers is worth a damn… There are some astounding tales to be told about the war which will make your hair stand on end when the facts are made public.

Lieutenant Raws believed his comrades were being murdered 'through the incompetence, callousness and personal vanity of those high in authority'. He died before Mouquet Farm fell; in all, 6300 Australians were wounded or killed in the drive to the farm.

Many soldiers came to see the generals as butchers—sending thousands to be massacred without a second thought—and bunglers, who planned botched battles in luxury, well behind the front-line, while their men suffered in the trenches. With little or no contact between the generals and ordinary soldiers, it was easy for the men to blame the commanders for failures. The war was meant to have been short, won using old military tactics of men marching in massed formations, but new technology had wiped out that hope and the generals, faced with a different kind of war, struggled to adapt. They tried new methods—creeping barrages, warfare in the skies, gas and massed artillery bombardments—but limited advances still came with horrendous casualties. The pressure was enormous—their governments and people at home wanted and expected a quick, decisive victory.

Despite 58 generals being killed on the Western Front—53 British, three New Zealanders and two Australians—most were well behind the front-line during battles. With wireless communication still in its infancy, it was difficult for the commanders to have a real-time understanding of what was occurring once a battle started; the phone lines were routinely cut, despite signallers risking their lives to fix them. Runners, carrier pigeons and flares were used, but these all had limitations—even if a runner made it through, it was more than likely that the course of the battle had changed before the generals could act on the new information.

On 5 September, the Australians withdrew from the Somme after being relieved by Canadian forces. In 45 days, since they had waited in the trench opposite Pozières, the I Anzac Corps had launched 19 attacks, the last seven in front of Mouquet Farm. According to Charles Bean, Australia's official war correspondent, Pozières 'marks a ridge more densely sown with Australian sacrifice than any other place on earth'. Over 23,000 Australians became casualties in those 45 days—resulting in calls for conscription to replace the losses. And although Pozières had fallen, Mouquet Farm and Thiepval hadn't—the one trench the Australian's had captured at the farm was retaken by the Germans three days later.

KILLED IN ACTION

PRIVATE EDWARD JENKINS
Bushman. 24 July 1916

SERGEANT DAVID BADGER
Bank clerk. 21 August 1916

LIEUTENANT JOHN RAWS
Journalist. 23 August 1916

CAPTAIN GORDON MAXFIELD
Accountant auditor. 3 May 1917

SERGEANT LEONARD ELVIN
Engine driver. 5 May 1917

CORPORAL ARTHUR THOMAS
Tailor. 8 June 1918

CHAPTER FOUR

THE SOMME, FLERS, 1916

IN MEMORIAM (extract)

To the men of the 3rd Battalion
N.Z.R.B who fell on the Somme

I am sitting in the shadows
I have borne the heat of day,
And I'm thinking of the comrades
Who have passed along the way.
They have scaled the furthest parapet,
Have crossed the Great Divide,
And are sleeping in their dugouts
Upon the farther side.

THIRD RESERVE

ON 12 SEPTEMBER 1916, the New Zealanders were welcomed by the sight of the dead as they crowded into the trenches at the Somme front-line, six kilometres from Pozières. In five days, they would take part in the British commander-in-chief General Haig's next major advance to capture the Germans' third defensive line, which included the villages of Morval, Gueudecourt and Flers. The New Zealanders were to capture three objectives: Switch trench, Flers trench and the Gird trench system behind Flers, an advance close to three kilometres. Instead of the narrow frontal advances the I Anzac Corps had faced, the New Zealanders would take part in a wide advance. With greater artillery than the Germans and a new secret weapon, the tank, Haig hoped for victory at the Somme before the winter rains arrived.

The ground was littered with swollen, sodden corpses. Fat flies crawled over limbs sticking out from the dirt, and pieces of bodies hung in the trees. A stench lingered in the air. In the trenches themselves, dead men lay beneath the mud, their bodies quivering as the soldiers stepped on them. On either side were the shattered remains of Delville Wood and High Wood. Haig had wanted them captured on the first day of the Somme battle, but they'd taken weeks of fighting to clear—the far end of High Wood was still held by the Germans.

At dawn on 15 September, sentries peered into no-man's-land as the sky paled. The soldiers had rum with their breakfast, and stared at the black trees of High Wood on the distant ridge. They'd had a bad night's rest; it was cold and they'd had to sleep in gasmasks. The men waited for zero hour and hoped to do their best. Two brigades were to follow a creeping barrage of shells that would leap forward 45 metres every minute. Each man was weighed down with a rifle, a bayonet, 220 bullets, two grenades, two empty sandbags, a waterproof sheet, a jacket, rations, filled water bottles, gasmasks, a steel helmet and a pick or shovel—36 kilograms in all.

Few expected to die, or even be wounded, but some believed there was a bullet with their name on it. Others had had premonitions of their death but still stood gripping their rifles as the artillery heralded zero hour.

At 6.20 a.m., four long lines of New Zealand troops, with British divisions on either side, followed the creeping barrage forward as German artillery gunners responded to their men's SOS. Shrapnel pellets and explosives dropped men in mid-stride. On their left, the Germans in High Wood held up the British, then turned their guns onto the New Zealanders advancing past the wood. Those closest to the trees, an Otago Company of the 2nd Brigade, were hit heavily; at the following roll call, only 34 soldiers out of 200 were unwounded.

Despite this, the New Zealanders stormed into Switch trench, shooting or bayoneting the few Germans who had time to react. They rolled bombs into the dugouts as the next wave of New Zealand troops passed over their heads, singing as they advanced towards Flers. Breaking into a charge, the second wave stormed Flers trench, bayoneting

German machine-gunners who'd fired until the last moment then tried to surrender. Dead and wounded Germans lay everywhere. In one dugout, several sat around a table with playing cards still in their hands, killed by concussion from an exploding shell.

With the second objective captured, the next wave of New Zealand soldiers 'hugged' the barrage towards Flers, waiting for each leap forward. They fought desperately in a sunken tree-lined road crowded with German dugouts. Some joined the British and followed a tank up the main street of the village. The tanks hadn't been as successful as hoped. Haig had expected them to replace the artillery, as well as terrify the Germans, but there weren't enough of them and they were still in their infancy. Of the 48 that started, most had broken down or been disabled by shellfire or the terrain. But the New Zealanders had been helped by two of the four tanks allocated to them: the tanks had trampled uncut wire and crushed troublesome machine-gun nests.

As New Zealand and British troops followed the tank through Flers, the Germans withdrew, releasing a pigeon with a note attached reporting the fall of the village. The Allied soldiers searched cellars and dugouts for prisoners, but, after a machine-gun crew surrendered and then opened fire, killing several New Zealanders, anyone surrendering was simply shot. Despite the tanks, the Germans had inflicted heavy casualties, and the Allies hadn't reached the Gird trench system or captured Morval and Gueudecourt. The New Zealanders had gained more ground than the British divisions on either flank, but in doing so had lost over 1800 out of 6000 men.

MANGLED AND TERRIBLE

For the next 19 days, the New Zealand Division stayed in the front-line. They shot down and shelled counterattacks and faced heavy shelling and gas. Flers was flattened, as were the newly captured trenches and a communication trench, nicknamed Turk Lane, being dug by the Maori Pioneer Battalion. Casualties rose.

Private William Gibbard wrote,

> The sights to be seen are terrible, mangled bodies lie everywhere, never shall I forget these sights, Mother, some of my best pals have gone this time.

Lance Corporal William Anderson was moving up to the front when he stepped over a body.

> The face was turned away but I recognised it as my brother. There was no halting as the Germans commenced lobbing shells in thick and fast.

Another New Zealander was killed beside his twin brother. After sunset, the soldiers buried friends and sometimes family in shell holes, dreading the letters they'd have to write home.

Heavy autumn rains flooded the trenches, and the one road to the front turned to thick liquid mud. Soldiers carrying supplies spent 11 hours travelling three kilometres. The Germans kept shelling the road as fast as the Maori Pioneer Battalion dumped rubble from nearby village ruins into the shell holes. Long lines of mules with artillery shells strapped to their backs struggled to the artillery crews. Drivers of supply wagons steered their horses around other dead beasts and upturned wagons. One horse, 'Finnigan', laboured on for five kilometres after being wounded by a bomb, only dying when he arrived at the front. Once the drivers had dumped their supplies, they carted away wounded men who cursed at every bump.

When the rain ceased, the New Zealanders continued to take part in small, localised attacks as well as large coordinated advances. In a major offensive on 25 September, the New Zealanders, with British divisions on either side, followed the most effective creeping barrage to date: it was so accurate and well timed that they got as close as 22 metres to the exploding shells. Germans trying to flee the fiery storm were mowed down by machine-gunners, and others were caught in their dugouts. Red flares, signalling success, filled the sky within half an hour. Many of the German prisoners were relieved to get away from what they saw as the 'Hell on the Somme'. There was success all along the line, and the Gird trench system and several villages were taken. The following day, 26 September, the British finally captured the long-sought-after Mouquet Farm and Thiepval village.

IT'S NOT WAR

The battles continued, all with the aim of breaking through the German lines, including a new fourth line. In one battle, heavy machine-gun crossfire caught the New Zealanders.

Australian ambulance men carrying their comrades, suffering from trench foot, to a transport to take them to hospital. AWM E00081

Bullets tore up the dirt in front of Lance Corporal Alexander Aitken, who'd served since Gallipoli, ripped his tunic, and whizzed past his ear. When one slammed into his arm, he dropped his rifle; his first instinct was to run away, but he resisted. He'd seen two other wounded men bolt from a shell hole in panic, and run in no particular direction until shot. When he was hit again in the ankle, he fell into a shell hole and waited there for the cover of dark before escaping.

In another battle, the New Zealanders attacked the Germans who'd defeated the Australians at Fromelles. They exploded 30 oil-filled Canister bombs above the German lines, which spat 'lurid flame'. Then the New Zealanders charged. One soldier, Private Kenneth Barr, ran with only one boot on—his other foot was swollen from a previous injury. They found the trench filled with German dead, piled high in places, scorched and disfigured by the burning oil. Some carried souvenirs taken from dead Australians.

Heavy rain fell again, and sentries stood knee-deep in liquid mud, their shoulders covered with oil-sheets, watching a bleak no-man's-land. On 4 October, after 23 days in the front-line, the New Zealanders tramped to a camp of tarpaulins set up on swampy ground. They were shattered, their uniforms in rags, greatcoats weighed down with mud and blood. One man had lost his pants and wore a 'sandbag kilt' instead. For many, the Somme was 'simply Hell on earth', as it had been for the Germans. Private Hector McLeod considered fighting an enemy soldier nothing compared to the artillery fire, which was 'not war, it's absolute murder'. For Second Lieutenant George Russell, the Somme was a 'mass of confused memories of heaps of men and bits of men lying about and of hills and villages and woods being torn to pieces'.

The New Zealand Division left the Somme and marched back to Armentières, where the locals greeted them as friends and mourned those who didn't return. Their part in the Somme offensive was over. They'd been in the line longer than any other division, captured 1000 German prisoners and eight kilometres of front-line three kilometres deep. But out of 15,000 men, 2000 had been killed and nearly 6000 wounded.

Newspapers in New Zealand printed lists of the dead, missing and wounded; in one paper the list covered two pages. After newspaper articles that glossed over the reality of battles, the awful truth about the war swept through homes. With the losses of Gallipoli still fresh, these new and far greater losses once again devastated whole towns. Sons, brothers, husbands, fathers and friends had gone to Europe 'from the uttermost ends of the Earth' and had died there. Their loved ones did not even have a body to bury. Whole communities went into mourning and some began to question the war. Even by 1916, Anzac Day had become a day of remembrance.

GOING INTO HELL

Although the Somme was finished for the New Zealanders, the offensive continued. General Haig wanted further advances of two and a half kilometres to gain higher ground before the winter rains arrived. He was convinced the Germans were losing their fighting spirit, but they were still managing to dig new defensive lines. On 7 October, the British advanced against troops forewarned of the attack by a deserter. The Germans mowed them down as they crossed the flooded land. A week later, men of I Anzac Corps, which had been stationed near Ypres in small dugouts with thin sheet-iron roofs, crammed into cattle cars, slid the doors shut to keep out the cold, and talked and sang around candles as they steamed down to the Somme. They were unimpressed; few wanted to leave the quieter Ypres area and some felt they were being thrown back into battle to save British soldiers. This was not the case; Haig simply considered the Australians to be in a fitter fighting state than the other divisions. The 5th Australian Division, which had been reinforced since Fromelles, was also ordered to the Somme from Armentières.

Icy winds cut into the men's faces on 21 October as they marched through Dernancourt, 16 kilometres from Flers, then past a sign for Fricourt stuck in the ground. It was all that remained of the village—even the rubble had been used to fill shell holes. In the valleys, British troops sang around small fires, or sat in dugouts, candlelight flickering through the blankets that covered their entrances.

Duckboard tracks took the Australians past Delville Wood, now nicknamed 'Devils Wood'. The dark hid the shattered trees and bodies but not the stench. As they moved up Turk Lane, arcing Very lights and flickering red shrapnel explosions lit the horizon. The dead lined the parapet, and wounded soldiers flowed back the other way. A passing British soldier told them, 'My God, you are going into hell up there.'

MUDDY RABBITS

When the duckboards ended, near the front, the men struggled through mud 'churned to the consistency of pea soup'. They passed a dugout in which officers were huddled around a box, reading a map by candlelight. The five-kilometre walk took seven hours, and after passing the ruins of Flers, the exhausted men took over the seized German trenches. Flares lit up severed arms and legs sticking out of the dirt walls.

As they waited for the next major offensive to advance the line, Whizz-Bangs caved in trenches, and blew fountains of mud in the air. The force of shrapnel explosions ripped clothes from the men. In the distance they could hear the staccato bursts of machine guns and the crack of sniper fire. The dead were thrown into shell holes and covered with slop. Soldiers went mad from the shock and tension—one man foamed at the mouth and crawled up the trench on all fours until he was removed.

When not on duty, the men took sanctuary in the German dugouts, even though their doors faced the German artillery. Those soldiers who didn't get a bunk slept on their packs. At least these dugouts were concrete; others were just holes dug in a bank or trench wall and, like 'muddy rabbits', the men crawled into them to sleep as 5.9s 'howled out of foggy space and burst with earth shaking fury' around them.

The rain and mud forced the postponement of the major offensive. Instead, smaller operations were ordered—on 5 November and 14 November—to seize a German salient and the higher ground that overlooked the Allied trenches. Despite brutal fighting, the Australians were driven out of the German trenches both times, leaving the men worn out and demoralised. Unable to bear it any longer, one or two Australians left their trenches and surrendered to the

Germans. Another soldier, learning he was to be sent to the front-line again, told his mates, 'I'm not going in—I'm finished,' then shot himself. Even out of the front-line, the soldiers slept in leaking barns on damp straw, without enough firewood to warm themselves or dry their clothes.

With the ground churned to slop by the endless rain, the six-hour walk from the rest camp to the front took 12 hours with men and pack mules constantly falling into mud-filled shell holes. Bogged animals had to be shot, and men dragged from the thick mud. One Australian officer had to be pulled out by a mule, and his back was broken. Exhausted or wounded men fell into the holes at night and died. Those lucky enough to have gumboots lost them as they struggled to get out; and some used corpses as footholds. Soldiers prayed for a 'blighty'—a wound that would get them out of the front-line. One man walked along the parapet in full view of the Germans, hoping to be hit.

In the trenches, the men stomped their feet to warm up, churning the ground even more. Unable to sit, they were on their feet all day and night. No fires were allowed, food arrived cold, and the tea, carried up in petrol tins, 'reeked so strongly of gasoline' that the soldiers joked it wasn't safe to light a match. Trench foot, caused by bad circulation, spread. If untreated, it turned to gangrene and often led to amputation. The soldiers were ordered to remove their boots regularly, rub whale oil into their feet and wear dry socks, but this was easier said than done. Soon, hundreds were being admitted to hospitals each week with trench foot.

SHEETS OF ICE

On 19 November, the battlefield conditions forced Haig to end the Somme offensive. The weather was a blessing for the Germans; it gave them time to recover and develop new defensive systems.

Since the battle had started, four and a half months earlier, over 500,000 British troops had been killed or wounded—the precise number their commanders had planned for. All that had been gained for those lives was an advance of eight kilometres. Although the French at Verdun had been relieved, the German Army hadn't collapsed and even the attempt to kill more Germans seemed to have failed—Australians patrolling in no-man's-land counted three British corpses for every dead German.

Gloomy drizzle settled over the land. The Australians stayed in the Somme trenches, peering through the winter grey towards the quiet German lines. The thinly held Allied trenches were almost invisible in the mud, and some carrying parties missed them, continuing on into German trenches. The back roads were slowly repaired, and materials arrived to fix the trenches. Eventually the men walked on wooden duckboards rather than mud, and sheltered under heavy sheets of iron. The New Zealanders took over the swampy land in front of Fromelles, manning strong points with nicknames like 'Windy Post' and 'Charred Post'.

In December, snow covered the land. Water in bottles froze solid, and hot tea iced over within a minute. Icicles hung from trench walls and helmets. It was the worst winter in 40 years. The men's hands and feet froze, and their thoughts turned to home and loved ones. They welcomed the sheepskin jackets and hot food delivered to the trenches and the cocoa and soup served in old jam tins at stalls on the way up to the front-line. Wrapped in layers of clothes, their greatcoats covered in frost, they burned anything they could get their hands on. In billeted barns they crowded around braziers, reading, writing or playing cards. They visited the warmer YMCA tents to chat, drink hot cocoa, write letters home or watch concerts.

The men loved getting letters from home, but Lieutenant George Mitchell recalled that 'the longer a man served, the fewer letters he got, the more he was forgotten'. Others complained that their letters had been lost or slowed down because of the submarine menace. Some sent letters home threatening not to write again until they received a reply.

It was a long hard winter, and many soldiers, like Mitchell, waited, knowing that 'some day there will be warmth, light and laughter—some day—for some of us!'

MORE WOODEN CROSSES

As the Australians and New Zealanders drained their trenches, brought in fresh bedding straw and tried to recuperate, reinforcements trickled in to rebuild the decimated battalions to fighting strength for the coming spring.

The French could tell immediately if a soldier was new or returning after a wound. The new troops all had the same 'happy, hopeful, young faces.' Once in France, New Zealand reinforcements were trained in bomb throwing and the 'spirit of the bayonet' at the 'bullring' at Étaples. The Australians were trained in their brigades. They were then transported to the front in cattle carriages with signs saying '40 men or 8 horses'. The journey was slow, and at each stop, troops left the carriages to stretch, buy alcohol or play two-up.

Closer to the front the mood changed, especially when hospital trains, loaded with the wounded, passed by. When Australian Sergeant Eric Evans, a new reinforcement, arrived at Messines in Belgium, 11 kilometres from Ypres, the sight of the many wooden crosses silenced him and the other new soldiers.

Once at the front, the reinforcements were split up and sent to different battalions and companies. The old hands—those who'd survived the Somme—did not give them a warm welcome; the new recruits were usually the first to be killed or wounded so no one wanted to befriend them. If they got any advice it was to forget all they had learned. New officers were trusted even less; most knew less about war than the men they were to command.

ANOTHER NEW YEAR

As the end of the year drew near, both sides tried to make the best of a bad situation. Despite several brutal raids, few shots were fired and the men were able to move about in the open more freely. But the Allies marked Christmas day by bombarding the German trenches. There was to be no repeat of the informal 1914 truce. As shells tore into the

Germans, the Australians and New Zealanders manning the front-line ate a 'bully beef stew, layered with ice, though sort of warm at the bottom', with a frozen orange for dessert that needed a bayonet to slice it. The Christmas pudding had to be thawed.

In February, as the frosts melted, 500 New Zealanders struggled across no-man's-land on a final raid before moving to Messines. With German SOS flares bursting overhead, the New Zealanders stormed the enemy trench, bayoneting, bombing and shooting in the darkness. As they returned, the German artillery smothered no-man's-land, killing and wounding many.

Stretcher-bearers returned to help the wounded, well aware that they made easy targets. But the Germans didn't fire. Instead, one soldier stood up in his trench with his hands raised to show they were empty. One by one, more Germans stood up, surrounded by their own dead comrades, and raised empty hands. The stretcher-bearers removed all the wounded they could find, then returned to their trench as a shot was fired, declaring the informal truce over.

KILLED IN ACTION

PRIVATE HECTOR MCLEOD
12 October 1917

CHAPTER FIVE

RABBITS IN HOLES, 1916

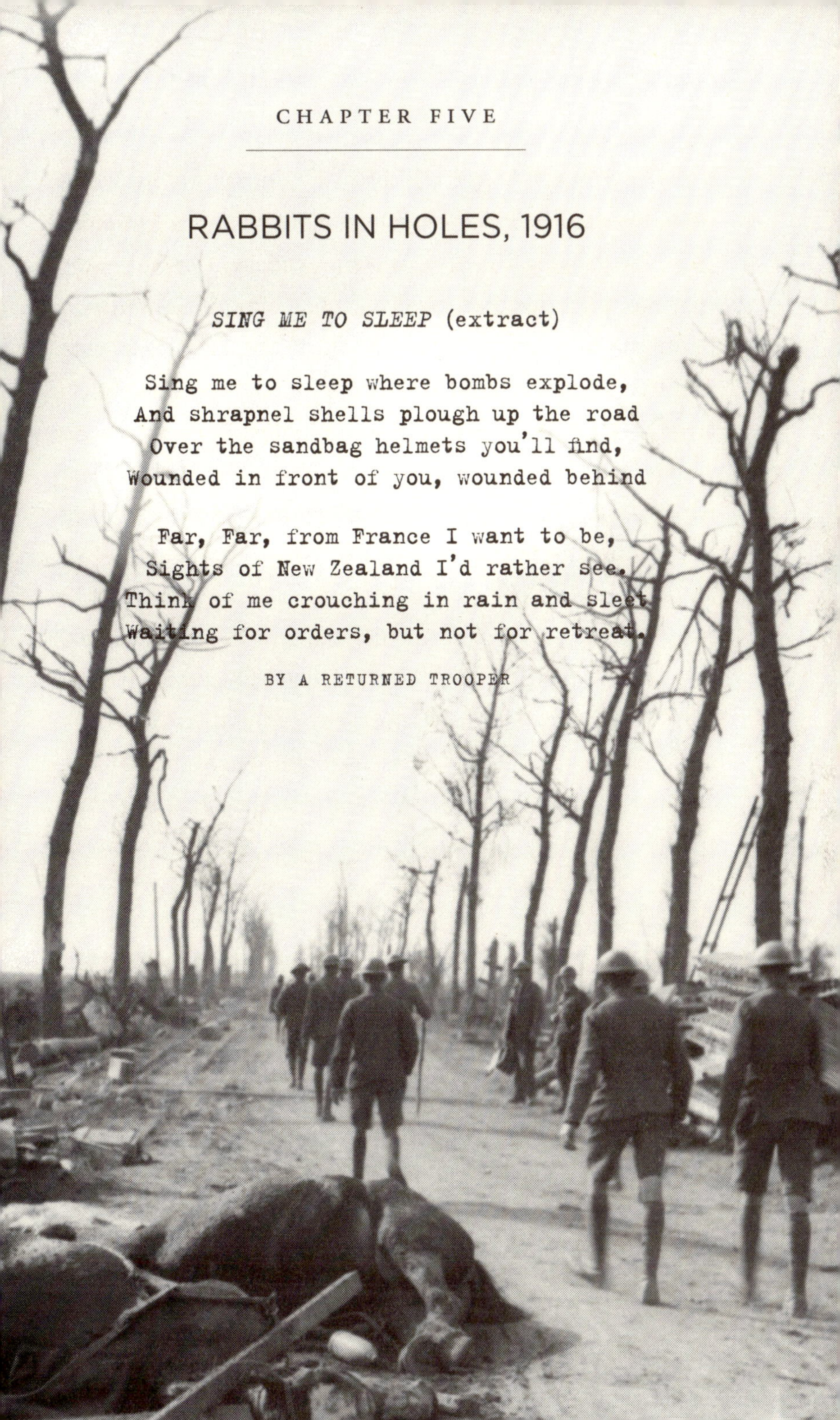

SING ME TO SLEEP (extract)

Sing me to sleep where bombs explode,
And shrapnel shells plough up the road
Over the sandbag helmets you'll find,
Wounded in front of you, wounded behind

Far, Far, from France I want to be,
Sights of New Zealand I'd rather see.
Think of me crouching in rain and sleet
Waiting for orders, but not for retreat.

BY A RETURNED TROOPER

WHEN SECOND LIEUTENANT Lindsay Inglis wrote home, he had little to say. 'Once more from the same old place. Still living the same old life, still fighting the same old war.' Days blended into weeks and months as the men followed the same routines. In their battalions, the men spent eight days in billets, four days in the subsidiary line, and four days in the front and support lines.

The first line of defence was the front-line. Although it was lightly held to prevent annihilating casualties during bombardments, the soldiers were still expected to hold off an attack until help arrived from troops in the support line, 130 metres to the rear. This fully manned trench was considered the strongest defence line. The subsidiary line, another fully held trench, was 450 metres further back, and was used as a semi-resting position before the men returned to their billets.

In the front-line, seven to eight men defended each bay in the two-metre-deep trenches, taking turns to monitor no-man's-land through periscopes—it was too dangerous to look over the parapet. Usually, little was seen of the Germans, or 'Fritz' as the Australians and New Zealanders called them, just the occasional grey-clad figure, or a dark silhouette moving in the distance. But 'Parapet Joe'—a nickname for the German machine-gunners who shot up the sandbags in front of the trenches—made sure they weren't forgotten. New Zealander Lance Corporal Ernest Williams found his first night in the trenches 'very quiet, the only thing we heard from Fritz being an occasional burst of machine-gun fire'.

At dusk, and again at dawn, the men 'stood to' for an hour with bayonets fixed to their rifles. Both sides used the grey uncertain light to launch attacks, as those charging could see the ground but might not be spotted until too late. At 'stand down', one sentry in each bay watched no-man's-land while the others cleaned rifles and had hot tea, bacon and bread for breakfast. During quiet days, they chatted, read, played cards, slept on the fire steps or in shelters, and wrote letters. At night—a more dangerous time—two men watched no-man's-land from each bay as the others waited or dozed, in full equipment, until their turn came.

Lieutenant George Mitchell felt that 'night crept slowly by. Time never lags so much as when in the front line.' Once, for entertainment, he practised firing single shots with his Lewis gun. Opposite him, a German soldier copied each shot. Mitchell fired off several shots in a rhythm. The German echoed them. Mitchell shot over a rifle grenade, saying, 'That shut the cow up.' But the German mimicked that too. After firing a phosphorous bomb, and hearing a 'terrible yell', Mitchell returned to his dugout to read. Not long after, three of his comrades ducked for cover as a phosphorous bomb exploded over their trench.

FATIGUES, PATROLS AND RATS

When not in the front-line, soldiers did fatigues—jobs required for the maintenance and defence of the trenches. They dug ditches for telephone signal wire, and took supplies like barbed wire, corrugated iron, pickets and ammunition up to the front-line. They also took turns on 'gas guard', and were extra alert when there was a wind from the east, which was signalled by windvanes on dugouts and trenches. Different gases had different odours, varying from rotten pears to mouldy hay to geraniums. When a suspicious smell was detected, the sentries banged on their empty shells and yelled 'Gas!' Soldiers scrambled to put on gasmasks and manned the fire steps, as church bells tolled and horns blew.

In the darkness, groups of soldiers slipped into no-man's-land to fix broken wire entanglements or to patrol. They passed 'advanced listening posts', in which several soldiers waited in shell holes to warn those in the front-line about enemy patrols or raids. Crawling on their bellies, they stopped and started, aware that the slightest movement or noise could draw attention to them. When the Germans illuminated no-man's-land with flares, the men froze and were mistaken for debris in the uncertain light. For Australian Sergeant Eric Evans, it was a nerve-racking time.

> Those damn flares constantly rising, hovering and fading, only to be replaced by yet more. Beautiful from a distance but deadly if caught in no-man's-land, as many a patrol has discovered. It was a chilly night but we were all dripping with sweat as we lay motionless and stranded.

Two or three patrollers, armed only with revolvers and Mills bombs, tried to locate shell-damaged enemy wire for future raids and prevent the Germans from carrying out their own patrols. They listened for digging in the German lines, which might indicate preparations for an advance, but often they heard nothing more than 'some snatches of indistinct talk or a burst of song in undertones'. They avoided enemy listening posts. If they were spotted, the Germans would alert their comrades with a 'low whistle' or 'the tinkle of a handbell', or perhaps just hurl a stick grenade at the men instead. If they ran into a German patrol, both sides would try to retreat secretly. If they couldn't, they'd fight a quick, brutal battle with revolvers and bombs before the survivors scurried away. If they came across a German wiring party, they returned to their lines, giving a password so they weren't mistaken for Germans, then passed on the wiring location to the artillery or machine-gunners, who targeted the area being repaired.

Each day, horse-drawn wagons carried up the next day's rations and ammunition, along with timber and iron for trench reinforcement. The supplies were dropped off at the side of the road for troops to carry to the front, along with food and hot tea from kitchens set up further back. In quieter, more established areas, the men pushed up supplies in carts on rail tracks, sprinting for their lives across exposed sections. On good days, the troops got hot tea three times, and in the evening, hot stew. At other times, the food delivery was more difficult. In his diary, Private Thomas Cleary wrote: 'Very short of tucker yesterday. Short again today. No breakfast...Very cold and miserable.' When water was scarce, men shaved and washed around shell holes, despite knowing there might be bodies in them.

The men's dugouts—often small shelters with a corrugated roof, surrounded by sandbags—became their homes, even if they leaked and couldn't withstand a direct hit. New Zealander Rifleman Alexander Hutton felt the men lived

> like rabbits in holes in the ground. It often makes me laugh to see all the heads poking out through the openings and to see how they disappear at any sign of danger in the shape of one of Fritz's shells.

At times, the incessant shellfire made it difficult to sleep,

Two soldiers look out of a dugout at the front-line, Hébuterne, France.
Alexander Turnbull Library G- 13190-1/2

as did the lice, which moved over the men's skin. Sergeant Evans found it impossible to sleep with lice 'gnawing' at him. 'They are tireless brutes. My skin is already red from itching.' He killed the eggs with a lit candle—another way was to run a thumb along the seams of clothes—and got 'satisfaction from the popping sound of burning them. But, like the "Huns", they don't know when to give up.'

Rats were everywhere, and they'd grown fat from eating corpses. They lived in swampy holes or the ribs of the dead in no-man's-land. They gnawed the men's packs and showed no fear of the living, at times stealing whole bags of rations.

With the endless duty of fatigues, some soldiers preferred being in the front-line. For Australian Sergeant Cecil Baldwin, it was the

> best of times...I did 3 hours work laying wire at night, and had the rest of the 24 hours to myself... We also had splendid tucker.

EGGS AND CHIPS

Moving to and from the trenches was often very dangerous. The German artillery had the approaches and the communication trenches well marked, so the men were relieved at night for safety. Two or three hours' walk would bring them to their billets, often in farms, and still within shelling range. '*Madames*' ran the billets, as well as the farms, while their husbands and sons were at the front. Unlike the officers, who got clean sheets, and breakfast at a kitchen table, the troops slept on straw, crowded into barns that stank of compost and manure.

At nearby villages like Armentières and Fleurbaix, the soldiers crowded into *estaminets*—cafes or bars—where *madames* and unmarried *mademoiselles* sold them coffee, wine, beer and eggs and chips. One tree-sheltered courtyard converted into a cafe was given the nickname 'Spy Farm' because it was only one kilometre from the front. The men flirted with the *mademoiselles* and joked about romance, but were always given the same answer: *'Apres la guerre'*—after the war. For many, these were the only women they saw or spoke to for weeks on end. Sergeant Cecil Malthus came to view one *mademoiselle* and her mother as his best friends.

A Maori soldier buying cakes from a local woman.
Alexander Turnbull Library G- 12755-1/2

THE CRUCIFIX

It was strange for the soldiers: one moment they were ducking from Parapet Joe, the next they were drinking watered-down beer, laughing, singing and briefly forgetting the war. The closeness of the *estaminets* to the front-line caused problems. At the beginning of the war, the humiliation of being sent home for misconduct was deterrent enough, but this threat wore thin after months at the front. Men went missing, fought, stole or turned to drink. New Zealander Sergeant John Russell drank to dull the memory of a raid he'd led:

> The yells were really pitiful and haunted me for some weeks...those blood curdling yells for which I was responsible, they made me feel most depressed for a long time.

At first, persistent troublemakers among the Australians and New Zealanders were sent to Field Punishment centres to do military training all day, often at a run. More serious offenders got Field Punishment No. 1—nicknamed 'the crucifix'—although the Australian commanders used it less. Early in the war soldiers were tied, spread-eagled, to a gun wheel for several hours a day over three days. Later on, they were tied to a pole. New Zealander Private Douglas Stark, considered a 'problem soldier', was tied to a wagon wheel in hot weather but still managed to raise his head to abuse any passing officer. Once, when a group of Australians tried to untie a man enduring Field Punishment No. 1, the major in charge threatened to machine-gun them down. At other times, rescuers were more successful.

In France, as in Egypt, the Australian soldiers quickly gained a reputation as larrikins with little respect for authority. They often refused to salute officers they didn't respect and had the highest rate of desertion among all the Allied troops. The Australian commanders responded with harsh prison sentences of up to 15 years long, but for some men this was a relief from the trenches. Small groups of Australian soldiers, often deserters, ran illegal gambling dens and looted, even using guns to resist arrest. Some Australian officers wanted the right to execute their soldiers, but the government, which wanted to introduce conscription, was afraid that people would oppose it if they knew there was a possibility the conscripts could be executed.

The New Zealand Army, under Major General Russell, on the other hand, did have the authority to execute soldiers, and Russell was prepared to do so, especially after an increase in disruptive behaviour. In the build-up to the Somme, Private Frank Hughes became the 'example to the rest'. He'd regularly left the front-line to get drunk. As 11 Maoris from the Pioneer Battalion faced him, their rifles loaded with either live bullets or blanks, Hughes refused a blindfold, saying, 'I want to see them shoot.' The officer sent to witness the execution had to turn his back. After Hughes' burial, French women left flowers on his grave.

The New Zealanders also executed Private John King, as well as Private John Braithwaite, who was a journalist and, as he put it, 'not a born soldier' but someone who'd 'answered the call'. His family had already had two sons killed and another two permanently wounded in the war.

The executions unsettled some of the troops. Lance Corporal William Anderson, who was in the same battalion as Private John Sweeney—another who was executed—thought he

> should have been sent in with the others to the Somme and given a chance of survival. It is likely enough the Germans would have provided the firing squad.

One soldier who was on Field Punishment was handcuffed to a tree stump after refusing to take part in the preparations 'to shoot a boy wearing the same uniform as himself'.

It wasn't surprising that some men couldn't cope. Lieutenant Mitchell recalled that there was

> something in trench-holding that is particularly nerve straining. One knows that, come what may, we must stay and take it...at the back of the soldiers mind is always that lurking feeling that the enemy artillery will concentrate on their trenches and wipe them with their garrison out of existence.

For Lieutenant Charles Alexander, there was nothing worse than to

> sit crouched day and night in a wet muddy trench and hear nothing but the scream of his shells...and to see your comrades...blown to pieces, dying of wounds in the mud and to realise that it may be your turn next.

Men ducked at the sound of shells, held their breath and tensed their bodies. Others found themselves shaking or twitching uncontrollably. Some deserted from the army, killed themselves, or shot themselves in their feet or hands so they could no longer fight. Those caught with wounds that appeared to be self-inflicted faced being disciplined.

Most had little choice but to continue—to not do so meant they'd let down their comrades and their own sense of honour. One New Zealand soldier, 'Clarrie', had insisted on going into battle with his company and was killed. He'd always been too terrified to fight so his commanding officer had given him jobs away from the front, for his own good and for those who had to share a trench with him. According to Second Lieutenant Ormond Burton, the

> really brave man is he who knows fear and overcomes it. Clarence had known it very dreadfully and to make things harder had fallen to it time and time again. Now he had the victory.

Others couldn't overcome the terrifying thoughts of death or injury. Private Victor Spencer, an 18-year-old who'd lied about his age when he'd enlisted, was the last New Zealander to be shot on the Western Front. After deserting with shell-shock, he was found living in a house with a French woman and two children. He said his nerves had 'been completely destroyed' and that he'd had to turn to drink. Out of 28 New Zealanders sentenced to death, five were executed. For generations, their families tried to clear their names; in September 2000, the New Zealand government pardoned them.

BLIGHTY

'A chap said to me today as we marched,' wrote Sergeant Evans, '"Kiss me Sergeant and make me sick, then I'll get blighty."' Getting a blighty, meant the men could be away from the front for two weeks to six months. Some wounded soldiers grinned as they were carted out. After losing his toe, Sergeant Malthus called, 'It's a blighty, a good blighty, it'll do me.'

At a casualty clearing station, Malthus waited with rows of wounded as doctors cleaned and dressed injuries. Those the doctors thought had a strong chance of recovery were loaded onto hospital trains, then onto ferries to England, where they went to overcrowded hospitals or to specialist units for their wounds. In one hospital, hundreds of men who had face wounds underwent experimental operations to clumsily reconstruct their noses and mouths. Many of the techniques were being used for the first time. In other hospitals, men who'd lost arms and legs had wooden, rubber and metal limbs fitted. Hospital wards stank of chloroform, pus and gangrene. Malthus almost died from blood poisoning when his wound became infected and gangrenous. After recovering, he, like others no longer fit to fight, sailed home.

Those that stayed were nursed back to health. Wealthy English aristocrats opened up their country homes for recovering soldiers, but with the welcome rest, memories of the front haunted them. Men woke sweating and screaming, babbling about their nightmares. Evans dreamed that he fell into a shell hole next to a wounded German, and they fought, but he didn't have a gun or knife, so he had to strangle the German.

Some who had missing limbs and smashed bodies wished they were dead. They saw no future for themselves. When the more fortunate had healed, doctors declared them fit to fight. Australian Corporal John Allan went back to the front with no illusions:

> No one who had actually gone through this war… witnessed its horrors is anxious to get back to it. I am going back. It is not from choice. It is my duty and that alone makes me go into it again.

A BLIGHTY VISIT

Every 15 to 18 months, the men were given clean, lice-free clothing and 10 to 14 days' leave to go to London, or sometimes Paris. With their leave pass, they boarded trains jammed with British, Canadians and fellow Australians and New Zealanders, then, at the French coast, boarded ferries for England and the white cliffs of Dover. Onlookers cheered as the troop trains sped through towns, en route to London. At Victoria Station, the men pushed through crowds of returning British soldiers being hugged by loved ones. When Lieutenant Mitchell arrived in London, he was 'vastly pleased with himself. Ten days of absolute freedom.' He swaggered onto the streets of London with an air of 'Make way for an Aussie on leave.'

It was an exciting time. There were no orders to follow, no fatigues, no flares or gun flashes; instead, the dimly lit streets were crowded with people. The Anzacs listened to the English accents around them and watched British soldiers having afternoon tea with their wives in tearooms. They slept in real beds between clean sheets on soft mattresses—'a glorious feeling' according to Second Lieutenant Burton.

They took guided tours or jumped on and off the tube and double-decker buses, visiting the famous London landmarks they had read or heard so much about: Westminster Abbey, the Tower of London, St Paul's Cathedral, the British Museum, Hyde Park. One by one, they ticked them off. In his diary, Sergeant Evans described how he strolled down Pall Mall to Buckingham Palace, swapped buttons with a Scots Guard soldier, and at Trafalgar Square saw the Queen Mother pass by in a car—'Though fairly old, she was still quite nice looking.' 'A simply ripping day, quite an Australian sunny day,' he wrote, aware that he'd been fortunate with the weather on his leave. Others found the climate gloomy, and couldn't understand why people would choose to live there when they could live in Australia or New Zealand. Many soldiers also visited family or the birthplace of their parents, once again concluding that their own countries were better.

The war was very evident in England. Food was rationed and men in khaki uniforms were everywhere. During air raids, the soldiers crowded into cellars with civilians until the all-clear signal was given. Private Melville 'Melve' King found it 'a pitiful sight to see women and children rushing among the streets of London looking for shelter from bombs'.

With food shortages and so many British men in France, the Anzac soldiers, with their distinctive swagger and high pay packet, had no difficulty befriending young women. They took them out to restaurants, then to movies and shows.

Other women, prostitutes, sidled up to the men, causing the army significant headaches. The soldiers—husbands and sons—had gone to fight for their country, but many ended up hospitalised with sexually transmitted infections. To stop infection, the Australian Army gave out condoms, but the New Zealand Army—reluctant to scandalise the public back home—preferred to give lectures. This approach led to the New Zealand troops having the highest rate of STIs out of all colonial countries fighting in the war. A New Zealand woman, Ettie Rout, who'd followed the troops to Europe against the government's wishes, handed out free condoms and set up a New Zealand–only brothel in Paris, until the army took her advice and began issuing preventative kits.

OLD FAMILIAR FACES

At the end of their leave, the men returned to France on trains that were quiet and dull compared to those that had taken them away from the front-line. Some overstayed, only going back when their money ran out. A few deserted for months; there were rumours that one soldier had joined the Irish Republican Army and that 'most of the bus and tram drivers in Ireland were New Zealanders and Australians'.

Although Lieutenant Edgar Worrall didn't fancy spending another winter in France, he returned to be back 'among the old familiar faces—or what are left of them'. As the war dragged on, the men's units and comrades became their family, and almost their reason to continue fighting. Soldiers returned to look for their mates to bury them, and gave up leave to visit their graves. Their friends died in their arms, and beside them during charges. Soon, they became friends with the next man they shared dugouts with or fought beside, until he too died or went missing. When shells fell heavily, the men talked to each other to ease the strain until the shelling had ended and they could return to sleep.

KILLED IN ACTION

SERGEANT CECIL BALDWIN
Accountant. 2 March 1917

LIEUTENANT EDGAR WORRALL
Medical student. 4 October 1917

DIED OF WOUNDS

LANCE CORPORAL ERNEST WILLIAMS
Lawyer. 29 December 1917

CORPORAL JOHN ALLAN
Dairy farmer. 3 October 1918

EXECUTED

PRIVATE FRANK HUGHES
Labourer. 28 August 1916

PRIVATE JOHN SWEENEY
Labourer. 2 October 1916

PRIVATE JOHN BRAITHWAITE
Journalist. 29 October 1916

PRIVATE JOHN KING
Miner. 19 August 1917

PRIVATE VICTOR SPENCER
Engineer. 24 February 1918

CHAPTER SIX

VOTE NO, MUM

GLASSINGTON—Died of wounds in France, April 6, 1918, in his 24th year, Private J. P. Glassington, dear loved husband of Myra, and father of little Jack and Millie.

Our home is always lonely,
Our hearts are always sad;
I miss my loving husband,
The children miss their dad.

NEWSPAPER 'IN MEMORIAM' NOTICE

BACK IN AUSTRALIA and New Zealand, friends and colleagues read the long casualty lists printed in newspapers or posted outside town halls, while families waited for the dreaded telegram that would inform them their loved ones were missing, wounded or dead. Later, a letter from a friend or officer would arrive from the front, explaining, where possible, how they had died or where they had last been seen. Often the families were told, the death had been heroic and quick.

From the beginning, those unable to fight had set up committees to collect bedding, clothing and money for the Belgian people and for the Red Cross. They contributed packages of cocoa, condensed milk and tobacco, home-baked cakes and hand-knitted socks, underwear and balaclavas to be sent to the troops. After finding out that a pair of socks lasted a soldier only two weeks, New Zealanders held a 'sock day'. To provide the fighting troops with basic comforts, which the army considered luxuries, committees organised shows and galas, workers donated a percentage of their wages, and school children raised funds by selling rabbit skins, leeches, frogs and firewood. Some of this money was used to set up hot cocoa and soup stalls for the soldiers. One group, the Otago Patriotic League, used its funds to have meat pies made and distributed close to the front-line.

Some women wanted a more direct active role. Although the Australian and New Zealand governments prevented women from being stretcher-bearers or ambulance drivers, female nurses served in hospitals and casualty clearing stations close to the front-line. Ten New Zealand nurses drowned in 1915 when their ship was torpedoed en route to Europe. At the front, they faced the same perils and conditions as the soldiers, and their stations were often shelled. During major advances they were overwhelmed with casualties. 'The Last Post is being played nearly all day at the cemetery next door to the hospital. So many deaths...' Australian nurse Sister Alice Ross-King wrote in her diary. Once, when her station was bombed:

> The noise was so terrific, and the concussion so great that I was thrown to the ground and had no idea where the damage was. I flew through the chest and abdo [abdomen] wards and called out: 'are you alright boys?'
>
> 'Don't bother about us,' was the general cry.

With the hospital lights out, and under a night sky full of searchlights and the roar of artillery, Ross-King found one of the tents collapsed. When she eventually found a way in, she tried to lift a delirious patient:

> I had my right arm under a leg which I thought was his but when I lifted I found to my horror that it was a loose leg with a boot and a puttee on it.

She was later awarded a Military Medal for her 'great coolness and devotion to duty'.

HOME WAR

As well as bringing together people back home, the war also created divisions. People with German heritage living in New

Zealand and Australia were abused and harassed. Some of them changed their surnames, while others had to quit their jobs. Anyone who had been born in Germany had to report to local police stations, and if they were considered a risk they were locked up in internment camps. The Australian government even changed town names—Germantown in New South Wales became Holbrook, named after a British Victoria Cross recipient.

As the war progressed, tensions grew. In January 1915, two Turkish sympathisers killed four and wounded seven people on a picnic train in Broken Hill, before being shot themselves in a 90-minute gun-battle with police and vigilantes. A mob, believing local Germans had agitated the two gunners, burned the local German club to the ground. In May 1915, a 5000-strong New Zealand crowd looted German-owned shops in Wanganui. In South Australia, Lutheran schools were shut down, and in New Zealand, Lutheran church bells were smashed and a church burned.

Eventually, the divisions broadened and new fractures arose; people even began to turn on those they believed weren't doing enough to support the war.

THE WHITE FEATHER

The heavy Somme casualties of 1916 cast a dark shadow over homes and communities in Australia and New Zealand. The enthusiasm at the outbreak of the war was evaporating, and, with fewer men now volunteering to replace the fallen, both governments raised the question of conscription, through which it would be compulsory for selected men to go to war.

At home, the sight of seemingly 'eligible men' who hadn't volunteered as soldiers angered many people, particularly those who had family at the front. Despite the initial rush to volunteer in 1914, most eligible men in New Zealand and Australia hadn't enlisted. There were many reasons for this: some believed it was unacceptable to kill; others felt the war was about profit and trade, not justice; some of Irish descent objected to fighting for England while it still controlled Ireland; and increasingly there were men who feared being killed or badly maimed.

After the heavy losses of Gallipoli, these men were called 'shirkers' or 'cowards'. Some were handed white feathers—symbols of cowardice—by women. The New Zealand Rugby Union banned anyone over 20 years of age from playing. A Bay of Plenty newspaper article suggested shirkers should be given the death penalty. People refused to work with eligible men, and some employers either sacked or refused to employ them.

After Britain introduced conscription in January 1916, many within New Zealand and Australia called for the same system, arguing that all able men had a responsibility to fight. Why should the shirker stay at home, they asked, while others died fighting for his freedom? Although both Australia and New Zealand had compulsory military training, it was for home defence only. Conscripting men to fight overseas was another matter.

THE BALLOT

In New Zealand the unions and the newly founded Labour Party opposed conscription, believing that more men would volunteer if soldiers' pay was raised to the minimum wage. 'War profiteering' by businesses had also increased; since 1914 food prices had risen by 16 per cent, but wages hadn't gone up. The Labour Party argued that if there was to be conscription of manpower, then the government should also conscript wealth, take over major industries, raise taxes to pay for an increase in soldiers' wages, and put an end to war profiteering.

Despite this opposition, the New Zealand government cautiously introduced conscription, telling the soldiers at the front and the British government that the New Zealand Division would be kept full 'as long as men are available'. The first ballot was held in November 1916. Using numbered balls dispensed by a machine, female clerical workers selected cards with the names of unmarried New Zealand men aged from 20 to 46. Unless two or more members of that family had already been killed in the war, balloted men were automatically conscripted into the army.

Afterwards, the rate of volunteering quickly fell; men waited instead to be conscripted. By 1918 almost all reinforcements were conscripts, and by the end of the war over 30,000 soldiers had been conscripted: one-quarter of the troops sent by New Zealand.

NO BLOOD TO FLOW

Although Maori men were not included in the conscription ballot, their enlistment numbers had also dropped after Gallipoli. At the outbreak of war, several prominent Maori leaders, including the politician Sir Apirana Ngata, had encouraged Maori to volunteer to prove their equality with the Pakeha—Europeans. At first, with recruitment numbers high, Maori volunteers were rejected—Britain didn't want 'natives' fighting Europeans—but as the war dragged on, this attitude changed. A Maori Native Contingent fought at Gallipoli, but on the Western Front, as the Pioneer Battalion, the Maori built roads and communication trenches. They wanted a combat role, not to be labourers, and this led to a fall in recruitment numbers. In February 1916, of the 314 'Maori' recruits, 203 were from the Pacific Islands.

The lack of Maori volunteers was also an after-effect of the 1860 Land Wars between Pakeha military forces and some Maori. These long-running battles over land ownership had effectively ended in defeat for the Maori, and the resulting bitterness and division were long-lasting. Those iwi (tribes) that had had vast tracts of their land confiscated by the government as punishment for 'rebelling', had decided not to fight for the British King. Now Iwi leaders who had supported the government during the Land Wars and had initially sent volunteers to the Great War argued that it shouldn't be only their men getting killed.

In June 1917, just as the first New Zealand Pakeha conscripts were arriving in England, the government extended conscription to the Maori, but only for its most vocal opponents—the Waikato Maori. Waikato leader Princess Te Puea Herangi immediately offered her pa as a safe place for those who'd been balloted but did not want to fight. The newspapers labelled them 'traitors'. When police entered the pa to arrest those who'd been conscripted, no one stood up when their names were called. The police arrested seven random men—one was 16 years old, another 60—and sent them to a military training camp. Of 552 Maori balloted, only 74 made it to the camp, and none went overseas. Those who continually refused to follow orders were sentenced to hard labour or put on bread and water diets.

RESISTING CONSCRIPTION

Belonging to one of three minor religious groups that opposed war before the outbreak of the Great War was the only way healthy conscripted men could avoid combat; even so, they were still expected to serve in non-combat roles. Men, Maori and Pakeha alike, who didn't want to serve, fled. Some went bush for the rest of the war; one man lived rough around One Tree Hill until he grew too weak to continue and gave himself up. On the West Coast, deserters lived in the hills above the mines. The miners left them food and warned them when the police were searching for them. One man joined the circus; many others stowed away on ships bound for the United States or Australia. One of those men, Robert Heffron, went on to become premier of New South Wales.

Despite laws making it illegal to speak out against conscription, opposition Labour members and other critics of the government still did. Paddy Webb, a Labour member of parliament for the West Coast, was sentenced to three months in jail for praising workers who went on strike because they opposed conscription. Then, in 1917, he was balloted to serve at the Western Front. Once balloted, men had a choice of serving or being imprisoned. When Webb refused to fight, he was court-martialled and given two years' hard labour planting trees.

Paddy Webb wasn't the first or last New Zealander to refuse to fight; 273 men were imprisoned by the war's end. They were given hard labour, forbidden to talk and then, when they had served their sentences, shipped to the Western Front to make it clear to others that prison wasn't a safer option than fighting. The government wanted equality of sacrifice; anyone who was fit and single was to fight.

'IT'S YOUR SUBMISSION WE WANT'

Archibald Baxter, a farmer from Otago, was one of those sent overseas after refusing both combat and non-combat roles. He was a pacifist who believed that if enough people refused to fight, governments would be forced to resolve conflicts peacefully. Like others, he claimed it was against his conscience to fight. After being balloted under the Family Shirkers Clause, which conscripted men from families in which no one had volunteered, Baxter was arrested and later put on a ship to England with other conscientious objectors.

Over the next six months, the army set out to break their beliefs. After being threatened with execution and given hard labour in the gruelling Dunkirk Prison, most agreed to non-combat roles. One soldier, Private William Little, agreed to be a stretcher-bearer, and later died from wounds.

Baxter was sent to France, close to the front-line, and was subjected to Field Punishment No. 1. The officer in charge tied the ropes so tightly that Baxter's circulation was cut off and his hands turned black. Frustrated by his continued resolve, an officer told Baxter that violence would be used until he was broken.

'What use am I if I am broken?' asked Baxter.

'It's your submission we want, Baxter, not your services.'

Baxter was sent to the front-line, where soldiers taught him when to duck shells, and saved his life when he tried to take off his gasmask too early. When an officer ordered four soldiers to repeatedly lift Baxter above their shoulders and drop him onto the duckboards as a punishment, the soldiers gently lowered him down instead, ignoring the officer's growing anger. Despite the kindness of some soldiers, Baxter began flinching at the sound of explosions. He collapsed in early 1918, and was declared mentally unfit for service. Before the end of the war, he returned home to his farm.

FORTY DAYS AND FORTY NIGHTS

Unlike New Zealand, Australia had not yet introduced conscription but after the Somme, the calls for it grew. The

Australian government held a referendum for the people to vote on it. The prime minister, William 'Billy' Hughes, had little choice; he supported conscription but he knew his governing Labor Party didn't.

Those who supported conscription believed every available man was needed to save Britain and therefore Australia. Those against felt that only a volunteer would give his fullest contribution. Some Australians also believed that the war was less about freedom and more about trade. Before the war, Germany had begun surpassing Britain as an industrial power—German companies controlled much of Australia's metals industry in 1914.

For 40 days and 40 nights both sides appealed to voters through public meetings, doorknocking, posters and badges. Some leaflets asked voters, 'Will you send another woman's son or husband to his death?' while others depicted ape-like German soldiers standing over a dead women, with the caption '"Your turn next". Help to prevent this by voting "YES."' The two sides clashed repeatedly; in one incident, hundreds of soldiers fought civilians who opposed conscription.

At the Western Front, journalist Keith Murdoch was concerned that the Australian soldiers would vote 'No' because they wouldn't want others to be forced to go through what they had experienced. Murdoch contacted the prime minister, who asked the Australian commander Lieutenant General Birdwood to persuade the men to vote for conscription. Birdwood and other prominent Australians appealed to the soldiers to vote for conscription, which a majority did, though it was soldiers who worked in the back camps and transports that swung the vote. But still the 'No' vote won in October 1916. The referendum spilt the community as well as the Labor Party, which expelled Hughes. But he continued to govern with several loyal ministers and the support of the opposition Liberal Party—together they formed a new Win the War Party. Without conscription, new methods had to be introduced to increase the volunteering rate. Returned soldiers, Victoria Cross recipients and mayors appealed to the public, calling for recruits during intervals at dances and shows, on beaches, and other areas where large crowds gathered.

These appeals saw 3000 men a month enlisting, but it wasn't enough—there were 38,000 Australian casualties in the last four months of 1917. In December 1917, a second referendum was held. This time the word 'conscription' was removed; instead, voters were asked whether they were in favour of reinforcing troops overseas. With Britain, New Zealand, Canada and the United States all using conscription, Hughes appealed to the public not to abandon the troops: 'Don't leave the boys in the trenches. Don't see them butchered. Don't leave them below their strength or you will cover Australia with shame.'

Tensions resurfaced. Minor riots broke out around the country and angry crowds filled halls to drown out speakers. In Melbourne, during separate demonstrations, returned soldiers and anti-conscription marchers attacked each another. Even the prime minister emerged with bleeding knuckles from the middle of a brawl at a train station. He had been talking to a 'Yes' crowd when an anti-conscription mob arrived and threw eggs, one of which hit him.

Not all returned soldiers were pro-conscription; several formed groups and published 'Vote No' leaflets. Private Victor Brown wrote home from France saying he didn't agree with conscription, as he and others considered it 'murder (or near enough to it) to compel anymore to come from Aussie', and that conscription would be 'the end of a free Australia'.

Pro-conscription leaflets claimed that those who voted 'No' were unpatriotic, that they believed men at the front should be sacrificed, women should be murdered, babies killed and Australia handed over to Germany. The anti-conscription league was just as emotive, appealing to families with posters saying 'Vote No, Mum, they'll take Dad next.'

The Australian people voted 'No' again. And although a majority of the soldiers at the Western Front had once more come out in favour of conscription, the number had fallen.

DIED OF WOUNDS

PRIVATE JOHN GLASSINGTON
Labourer. 6 April 1918

PRIVATE WILLIAM LITTLE
Miner. 4 September 1918

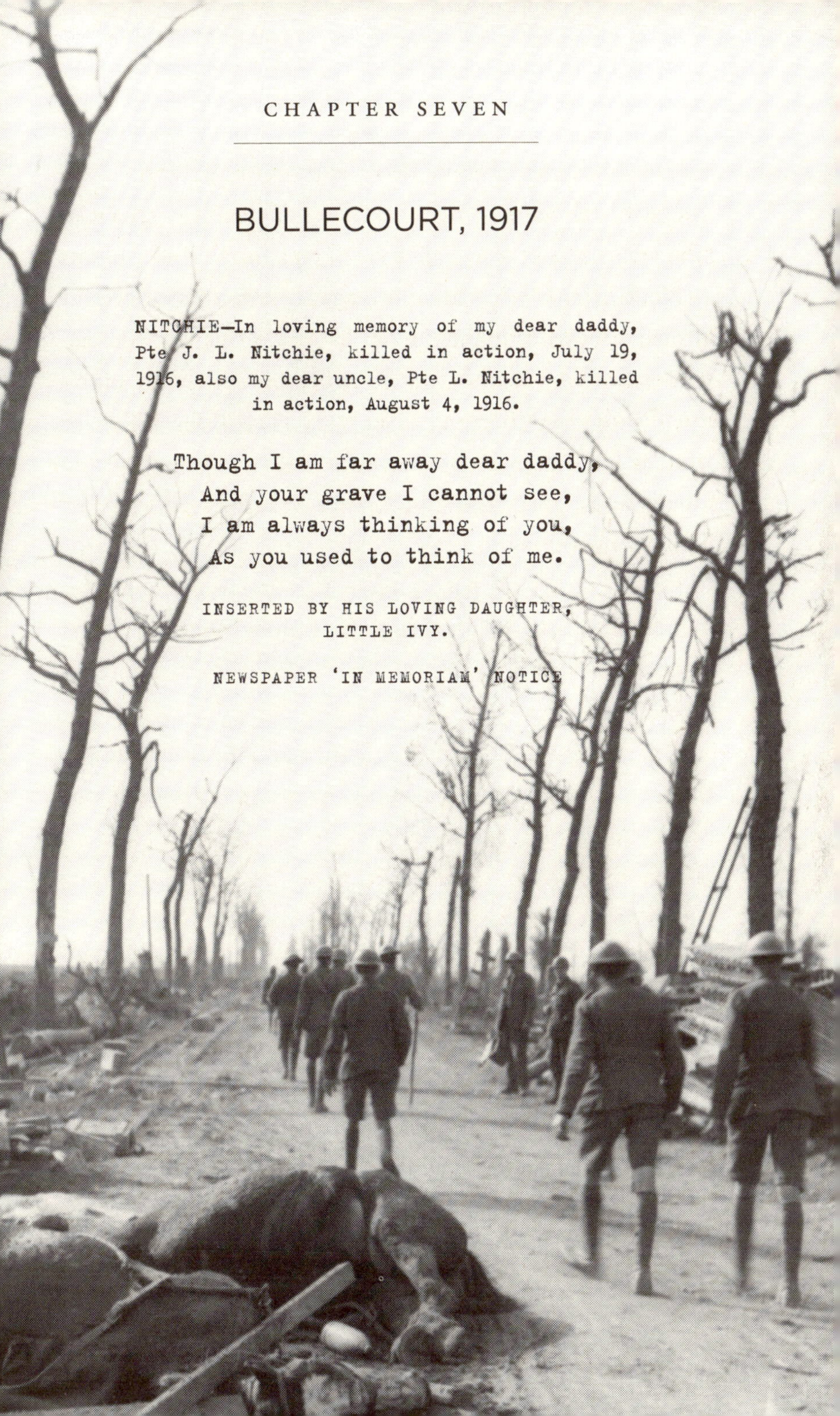

CHAPTER SEVEN

BULLECOURT, 1917

NITCHIE—In loving memory of my dear daddy, Pte J. L. Nitchie, killed in action, July 19, 1916, also my dear uncle, Pte L. Nitchie, killed in action, August 4, 1916.

Though I am far away dear daddy,
And your grave I cannot see,
I am always thinking of you,
As you used to think of me.

INSERTED BY HIS LOVING DAUGHTER,
LITTLE IVY.

NEWSPAPER 'IN MEMORIAM' NOTICE

WITH THE SPRING of 1917 approaching, Haig—who now held the rank of field marshal—reluctantly agreed to take over parts of the French line. The aim was to support a French offensive further south against the wooded heights of the strongly held Chemin des Dames. After the bloodletting of the Somme, the French commander-in-chief General Joseph Joffre had been replaced by General Robert Nivelle, who believed in victory through 'violence, brutality and rapidity'. Haig's British troops were to attack between the Somme and Arras to draw German troops away from the French. Haig would have preferred to attack the Germans in Belgium, but the British prime minister, David Lloyd George, had lost faith in him after the senseless slaughter of the Somme.

Since August 1916, the Germans had also been making changes. After General Falkenhayn's failure at Verdun, the Kaiser had replaced him with Generals Paul von Hindenburg and Erich von Ludendorff. They'd decided to create strong defensive positions rather than recapture lost ground or attack fortified positions as Falkenhayn had done. After halting operations at Verdun, Ludendorff ordered the building of a new defence line, known to the Allies as the Hindenburg Line. The new trench system, up to 40 kilometres behind the Somme trenches, ran from Reims to Arras. It straightened the original line, which reduced the number of men needed to defend it.

On 24 October, French forces led by Nivelle had counterattacked at Verdun and by December had recaptured their lost forts. In the same month, the Germans offered the Allies a peace deal in which they would keep Belgium—it was immediately rejected. Then, in January 1917, they relaunched their unrestricted submarine campaign, which they had eventually halted after American outrage at the sinking of the *Lusitania*.

THE GERMANS ARE GONE

By February, with the Hindenburg Line nearly finished and the winter frosts melting, Australian patrols discovered the Germans trenches on the Somme empty. They were withdrawing across a 210-kilometre front—setting fire to villages, mining roads and leaving machine-gun posts at strategic locations to slow the pursuing Australian and British soldiers. The Germans, some wearing looted suits or dresses, toppled house walls, tore tiles from roofs and cut down trees. Nothing was to be left for the Allies.

Even so, the Australians' spirits lifted: the worst of winter was over and the Germans had withdrawn. After 10 months of trench warfare, the men were fighting out in the open and, although it was just as brutal, they felt for the first time that they were winning the war. They passed through the burning town of Bapaume, leaving the wasteland of the Somme behind them. They fought desperately, capturing village after village until they were halted by the chalk-white parapet and deep wire rows of the Hindenburg Line.

As drivers manoeuvred horse-drawn artillery over sabotaged roads, the 4th Australian Division moved forward to take over the new front-line. They passed the bodies of Australians killed in the pursuit—some buried in German-dug graves—and hospital trains filled with wounded men going the other way. Then welcome news arrived: finally, on 6 April, the United States had declared war on Germany. The Germans' return to unrestricted submarine warfare had been the last straw.

THE BATTLE OF ARRAS

On 9 April, the Allies began their planned offensive at Arras, close to where the Hindenburg Line joined the original German line. British and New Zealand tunnellers had hacked over 32 kilometres of tunnels and chambers through the chalk ground under Arras, and as an artillery barrage crushed the German defenders, 30,000 British troops moved secretly through the tunnels to the jumping-off point. Nearby, Canadian soldiers also readied themselves.

At zero hour, the Canadians stormed the strategic heights of Vimy Ridge, while British troops smashed through the line at Arras, but any further attempts to exploit the break were shut down by desperate German fighting.

Twenty kilometres from Arras, General Gough, commander of the 5th Army, ordered the Australians to attack Bullecourt village, a bastion built into the Hindenburg Line, to both support and take advantage of the Allied gains. However, the double belts of wire—specially angled to direct attacking troops into the line of fire—were still intact, so Lieutenant General Birdwood asked for a postponement.

Gough told him that a line of 12 tanks would do the job of the artillery and crush the wire. For a long time tank commanders had wanted to attack en masse—now they had their opportunity.

At 4.15 a.m. on 10 April, soldiers from two brigades of the 4th Division lay on the snowy ground listening for the tanks, as 'grape-like bunches of coloured lights' hung momentarily over the German line. On their left, a brigade of the 62nd British Division was to pass through Bullecourt once the Australians and tanks had cleared it. Beforehand, British patrols would also support the advance by attacking the Hindenburg Line on the other side of Bullecourt, but this was not known to the 4th Division front-line troops. By dawn, not one tank had arrived, so thousands of Australians stood up and strolled back to their trench, 'like a crowd from a football match', luckily concealed by snow flurries. The British patrols ran into uncut wire and machine-gun bullets. Those who survived were bitter that the Australians hadn't told them the attack had been postponed.

THE 'MONSTERS'

After resting during the day, the same tired soldiers got back into position on the snow-covered slopes as the British gassed Bullecourt. One of the reserve soldiers, Private Wilfred Gallwey, was so exhausted that he could only drag his rifle. His knees were giving way, and he wondered 'of what use would I be tonight'. Again Birdwood tried to have the attack postponed, but Gough insisted that Haig expected them to proceed. This time, the tanks were there. At 4.45 a.m., zero hour, their overheated exhausts glowed red as they churned across no-man's-land with long, straight lines of soldiers following. Many Germans fled from the 'monsters', but those that stayed kept firing. Bullets hit the tanks, causing 'metal splash': bolts, solder, thick paint flakes and rivets were torn off the interior walls and spat into the crew space, gashing or blinding the men inside. The German artillery, mechanical failure and boggy terrain crippled most of the tanks before they had even reached the wire—only four made it, but they were so slow that the Australians had overtaken them.

German SOS rockets lit the night and the replying artillery shells tore into earth and men alike. Gas clouds billowed towards the British and the 4th Division and, up ahead, dead and maimed troops were hanging in the uncut wire. One soldier thought that the wire 'seemed to swarm with fireflies' as bullets struck it. But the Australians scrambled through gaps and captured the main trench and the support trench, then barricaded the ends and dug fire steps in the other side of the trench wall. Captain Harry Murray sent runners with messages saying they were 'in' and could 'keep the position till the cows come home' if they had artillery support. But the artillery remained silent. The commanders mistakenly believed that the tanks and troops were advancing past the trenches, and they wouldn't risk shelling their own men.

Without an artillery barrage, German soldiers were able to creep close to the barricades, with bombs, while others shot at the Australians from nearby houses. Private Gallwey could 'only describe it as Hell. Every minute I expected to be blown out...All around me men were falling...' The Australians released pigeons with messages demanding more ammunition but the bullets sweeping no-man's-land prevented reinforcements and supplies getting through.

By 11.30 a.m., with bombs exploding around them and their own running out, Murray gave the order to withdraw. Corporal James Wheeler, in charge of one outpost, was unsure where the order came from so he told his men to stay and 'fight it out like Australians'. They were captured, along with other posts who stayed to fight. Murray now urged those men around him to 'run the gauntlet back through the wire..."There's two things now," he said, again and again, "Either capture, or go into that!"' The wire sparked with the hum of bullets. Other officers told their troops, 'Every man for himself.'

Few of those that tried to escape made it back. Lieutenant George Mitchell was one of the last to try, and as he left he felt the heavy gaze of the wounded. 'You are not going to leave us?' one man pleaded. Mitchell and another 150 Western Australians walked out slowly and deliberately, supporting newly wounded men, through the bullets. Mitchell had promised to send back stretcher-bearers for those left in the wire, but it couldn't be done. Along the line, over 1100 Australians chose to surrender. One soldier whose foot had been blown off waited for the Germans with a Mills bomb in his hand.

By noon, the battle was over and the Australians watched

A tank going into action near Messines, Belgium.
Alexander Turnbull Library PA1-f-091-H391

German troops help the Allied wounded in the wire, or shoot those beyond help. For two hours, both sides respected an informal truce as stretcher-bearers retrieved their wounded. When snow began falling, the Germans called out 'Finish hospital' and the men returned to their lines.

Mitchell and others stumbled back towards their camp. They were utterly exhausted and barely able to stand, so they staggered into an abandoned factory beside the road, built a fire with window frames and drank tea made from melted snow. Mitchell fell asleep in a bed he made from German coats.

The 4th Division had been the first to storm and hold the new Hindenburg Line, but at a great cost—over 3000 had been killed, wounded or captured. In Mitchell's battalion alone, only 42 men out of 630 were left standing. The attack with tanks had failed miserably and the Australians' confidence in the British command had been further shaken; it was a long time before they fought willingly alongside tanks again.

Four days later, on 15 April, 4000 men of the 1st Australian Division holding a one-kilometre sector next to Bullecourt were attacked by 16,000 Germans troops, whose commanders wanted them to destroy the artillery and as many men as possible, then withdraw. The Germans overran the lightly held front-line and 21 guns, but an Australian counterattack drove them back. Over 1000 Australians were killed or wounded; 2000 Germans lay dead or wounded and 362 had been captured. The German POWs were sent back to wire cages or labour camps, where, after having their details taken, they were fed, and were allowed to write home, but only about their health and general treatment. Afterwards, they were used as labourers to repair roads and other infrastructure.

LAMBS TO THE SLAUGHTER

The following day, the French attack at the Chemin des Dames failed miserably. The Germans had found battle orders for the attack on the body of a dead despatch-rider and, knowing the day and the time of the attack, had mowed the French down. The French soldiers began to mutiny, complaining that they were being slaughtered because their generals had no idea what they were doing. Young draftees marched through a village baa-ing like sheep being led to an abattoir. Large numbers of troops in the front-line refused to follow orders; others stationed in towns behind the front refused to return to the line. There were fears that France was on the brink of revolution and that, if Germany discovered that the French line was in disarray, the war could be lost then and there. Mass arrests and mass trials followed, but the new French general Henri-Philippe Pétain also decided to cease attacks until the troops' strength and spirit improved, and the Americans arrived. This increased the pressure on the British and other Allies enormously; they were now responsible for winning the war and for diverting German attention away from the problems with the French line.

A new British attack was ordered for 3 May. On the extreme left of a 25-kilometre front—the widest Allied advance yet—the Canadians would attack from Vimy Ridge, while on the extreme right, the 2nd Australian Division would attack to the right of Bullecourt. It was the same plan as last time, except that instead of tanks the Australians would follow a creeping barrage, seize the Hindenburg Line, then push on for 800 metres and take the village of Riencourt—in all, a 2700-metre advance. The 62nd British Division to their left was to capture the rubble heap of Bullecourt.

Above the soldiers, brightly coloured biplanes and Sopwith triplanes were fighting in the skies. The Albatros biplanes were part of Captain Manfred von Richthofen's 'Flying Circus'. He was nicknamed 'the Red Baron'—red after the colour of his triplane. In April alone—'Bloody April', as it was called by the Royal Flying Corps—Richthofen shot down 22 aeroplanes. With German pilots winning supremacy of the skies, their spotters observed the battle preparations below. One day before the attack, a downed German pilot asked his Australian captors 'What time is zero?' The Germans knew an attack was coming; they just didn't know the exact day or time.

BAY BY BAY

The full moon was so bright on the night of 2 May that the 2nd Division sheathed their bayonets to stop the moonlight reflecting off them. When it sank, they moved to the jumping-off line to wait for zero hour. The 6th Brigade was on the left, closest to Bullecourt, while the 5th Brigade was on the right. A sunken road that ran from their line through to the Hindenburg Line separated them.

At 3.45 a.m. the drum-roll roar of the creeping barrage erupted. Unsheathing their bayonets, the Australians marched forward. The dead from the April attack still hung in the wire. On the right of the sunken road, the Germans spotted the 5th Brigade, and, despite shells exploding around them, the Germans opened fire with such intensity that an Australian officer panicked and yelled at his men, 'Pull out—retire—get back for your lives.'

On the left of the sunken road, the 6th Brigade scrambled into the first and then the second German trench the

PILOTS

Australian and New Zealand pilots flew with the Royal Flying Corps or, from September 1917, with one of three Australian air squadrons stationed in France. The pilots—some of whom had already served as infantry in the trenches—flew in open cockpits, exposed to the weather. They carried out bombing raids and surveillance work, flew over German artillery positions directing their own gunners to destroy the gun-pits, bombed and machine-gunned enemy troops and engaged in dogfights with German aeroplanes.

Fighter pilots flew in single-seater biplanes and triplanes with a machine gun that fired through the propellers. Surveillance aeroplanes were two-seaters; the observer sat behind the pilot with a machine gun.

Although training to fly the new inventions was as dangerous as combat—over one-third of pilots were killed in training accidents—many feared the day they would fight. Australian fighter-pilot 'ace' Captain Arthur 'Harry' Cobby would have done anything to delay going into combat. The dogfights were chaotic, and no sooner would a pilot have an aeroplane in their sights than there would be 'the old familiar "pop-pop-pop-pop"' of a German pilot getting into position behind them. An moment the barrage lifted. They rolled bombs into the dugouts—the speed of the attack caught the Germans still inside—then slowly bombed the trenches towards Bullecourt, which the British had failed to capture. At a cross-trench, the Germans sheltering in a dugout had set up a machine gun and, with an ample supply of bombs, fought

observer described the dogfights as being:

> every man for himself. We go hell-for-leather at those snub-nosed, black crossed busses of the Hun, and they at us...Hectic work. Half-rolling, diving, zooming, stalling, "split-slipping", by inches you miss collision with friend or foe. Cool precise marksmanship is out of the question.

In one battle, Lieutenant Percival Schafer escaped an attack by three red German Albatros D.III triplanes, returning with 62 bullet holes in his machine.

Major Keith Caldwell, flying with the British, was New Zealand's leading ace, with 25 victories. In 1917, pursued by a crack German pilot, Caldwell pretended his Nieuport biplane had been hit, and spun to the earth, only just pulling up at the last second. On another occasion, when his machine was cork-screwing towards the ground after a wing strut was damaged by a collision with an Allied biplane, Caldwell stepped out of the cockpit and onto the wing. Grabbing the damaged wing strut, he levelled his machine with one hand, using the other to steer it back over the British line. At the last second, just before it hit the ground, Cadwell jumped clear, to the astonishment of the watching British soldiers.

to stall the advance. The fighting for each bay was fierce and violent. Led by Lieutenants John Jennings and William Braithwaite, the Australian bombers threw captured grenades as well as their own. Bombs blew off Jennings' fingers and wounded Braithwaite in both arms, but they didn't stop. As Stokes mortar bombs rained down, the Germans pulled back to another dugout entrance to continue the fight.

The attack was failing. Only the 6th Brigade had got into the Hindenburg trenches, and they desperately needed support. On the other side of the road, the 5th Brigade launched a bombing attack up the German trench, led by an unknown officer in a grey cardigan. His steel helmet and jacket discarded, the officer clambered out of the trench into the open to throw bombs, forcing the Germans back up their trench. Slowly, bay by bay, they were winning with bombs what they'd failed to capture by charging. But at 7.45 a.m., when the officer fell, the fight turned and the Australians were bombed back to the road. After hurriedly barricading the trench mouth, they fired mortar after mortar horizontally, like rockets, down the trench. When the Germans retreated, six volunteers gave chase with bombs and after retaking the section of trench just lost, they barricaded it with sandbags and dead bodies.

Over the next 13 hours, the Australians lost and recaptured this section four more times, fighting all day until the sun set and German flares lit the dust-blurred night. Fit men had little choice but to leave the wounded to fend for themselves. One corporal with shrapnel in his knee piggybacked a more seriously wounded soldier to a field hospital. Another soldier, with a gaping hole in his stomach, replied to his officer's encouragement to 'Stick it out, lad', with 'Don't worry about me, Sir, but give the bastards hell!', then put his rifle between his feet and shot himself. Just after midnight, fresh troops from the 1st Division relieved the exhausted soldiers. At the end of the first day of battle across a 25-kilometre front, only the Canadians on the left and the Australians on the right still held any captured ground.

At dawn, British troops made a second attempt to capture Bullecourt. The Germans had been living in deep dugouts hidden so well under piles of rubble that even their own supply parties struggled to find them, leaving those in the village to survive on rations taken from the British dead. German sentries watched for attacks from the entrances and, at the dawn 'stand to', the soldiers crowding the stairs spotted the British advance. They poured out of their dugouts, lay down, and destroyed the attack.

PULLING PINS

Fresh troops of the 1st Division massed in the sunken road and waited until midday for their turn to drive the attack up the trench on the right.

On either side of the road, no-man's-land was littered with the dead, dying and wounded. When stretcher-bearer Corporal Granville Johnson noticed a wounded man waving a handkerchief near a disabled tank, he begged his officer to let him rescue the man. As he walked out with fellow stretcher-bearer Private Harold Ringland, a German riflemen and a machine-gunner opened fire. Bullets tore up the ground. The Australians got the wounded soldier onto the stretcher, but as they carried him back, Ringland was killed. Twenty-four-year-old Private Arthur Carlson raced out and helped carry in the stretcher. When other wounded men called for help, Carlson risked the bullets three more times. As he bandaged a man's wound out in no-man's-land, another stretcher-bearer, Private James Paul, tried to help him but was killed. From shell hole to shell hole, Carlson carried the wounded man until hit in the hip by a bullet. Refusing to give up, he crawled back, dragging the man with him. His actions raised the spirits of the Australians, but also created more bitterness towards the Germans, who would have known they were shooting at unarmed stretcher-bearers.

The 1st Division chased the exploding shells up the trench, keeping close to the German bomb-throwers so their stick bombs would explode harmlessly behind them. They fought stripped to the waist. Lieutenants John O'Connell and John Moy, with revolvers in one hand and bombs in the other, pulled the pins with their teeth before hurling the bombs into the next bay. Whenever the German bombs subsided, two 'bayonet men' and the lieutenants rushed around the corners, shooting and stabbing any Germans left alive. For four hours they bombed and shot their way from bay to bay, trampling and tripping over a carpet of Australian and German dead. Reaching the same barricades built and lost by the 5th Brigade the day before, the exhausted bombers stopped.

HOLDING ON

The 1st Division now held over 1000 metres of the Hindenburg Line. As the British attacks ended, newspaper headlines and the world's attention focused on the Australians at Bullecourt and the fighting that continued for the next 12 days. All through the night of 5 May, German shells shattered posts and buried men alive as their troops attacked the barricades, but the Australians held them back. On 6 May, 80 German soldiers and bombers advanced behind a flamethrower, the roaring flame burning up the dark. Most of the Australians ran, but Captain Alexander MacNeil hid until the flame had passed, then killed the flamethrower with a well-timed bomb. When MacNeil left the trench to bomb a second flamethrower, he was cut off, and panic spread through the remaining Australians as the Germans advanced towards them and the sunken road.

When 24-year-old New South Wales builder Corporal George Howell saw the retreating Australians, he rushed across the road, then ran along the parapet, throwing bombs down onto the Germans. After jumping into the trench, he attacked with his bayonet. The Germans scrambled back, chased by those Australians who'd initially fled. They leaped over the badly wounded Howell, who'd single-handedly stopped the German advance, and didn't halt until they'd recaptured the section of trench just lost. For his actions, Howell was awarded a Victoria Cross, the highest military award.

The battle for Bullecourt eventually required the 5th

Australian Division as well—the third Australian division used—and continued until 17 May, when the Germans decided it was no longer worth holding Bullecourt and retreated. Field Marshal Haig's plan to distract the Germans while the French recovered had gained little except the killing or wounding of 7000 Australians and thousands more British and Canadians. Nine days later the last Australians withdrew from the Hindenburg Line, exhausted and in desperate need of rest and reinforcement for Haig's fast-approaching Belgian offensive.

KILLED IN ACTION

PRIVATE JAMES NITCHIE
Labourer. 19 July 1916

PRIVATE LESLIE NITCHIE
Barman. 4 August 1916

LIEUTENANT JOHN JENNINGS
Commercial traveller. 3 May 1917

PRIVATE HAROLD RINGLAND
Clerk. 4 May 1917

PRIVATE JAMES PAUL
Farm hand. 4 May 1917

CORPORAL GRANVILLE JOHNSON
Shop assistant. 11 September 1918

LIEUTENANT WILLIAM BRAITHWAITE
Tanner. 3 October 1918

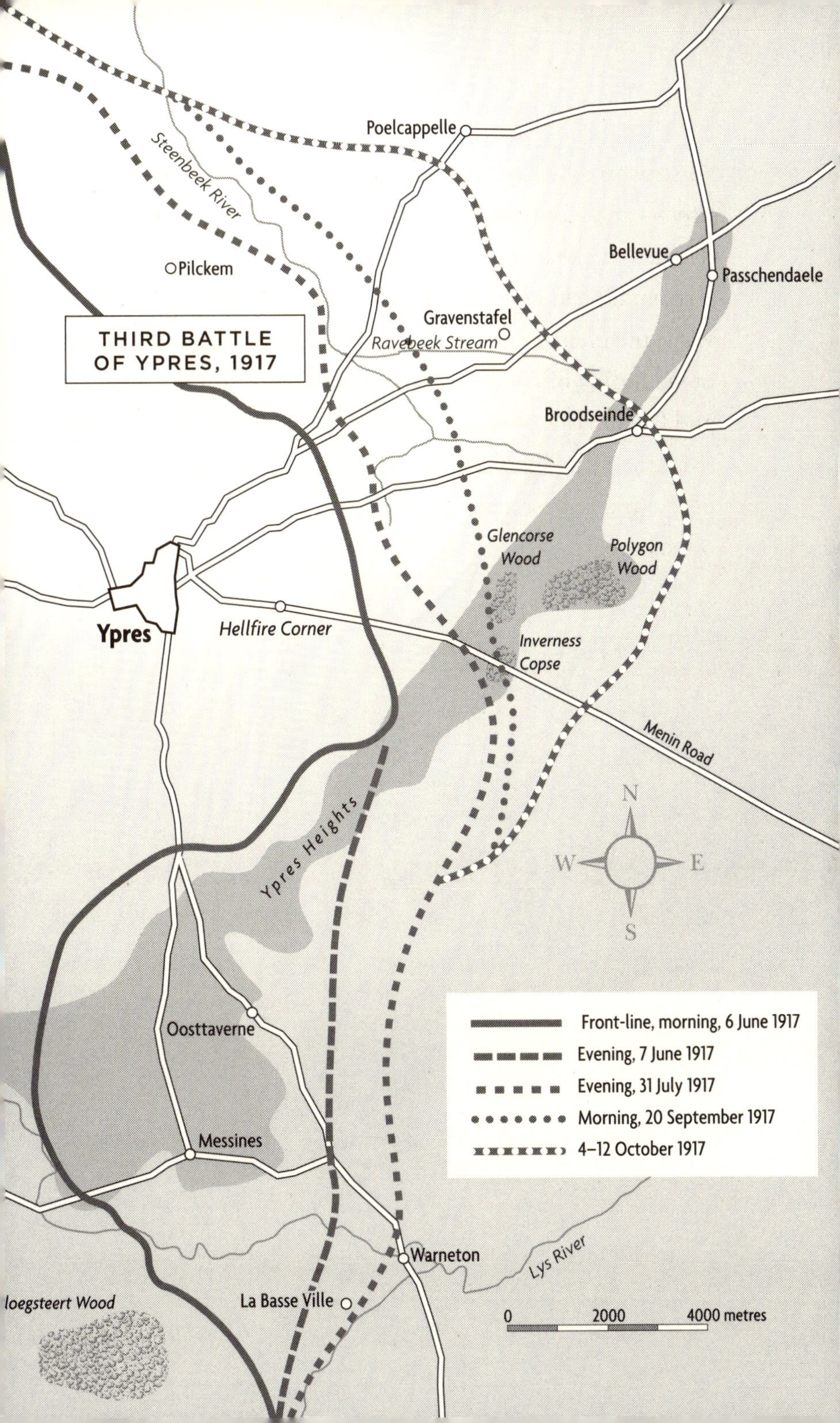
THIRD BATTLE OF YPRES, 1917
Poelcappelle
Steenbeek River
Pilckem
Bellevue
Passchendaele
Gravenstafel
Ravebeek Stream
Broodseinde
Glencorse Wood
Polygon Wood
Ypres
Hellfire Corner
Inverness Copse
Menin Road
Ypres Heights
N
W
E
S
Oosttaverne
Messines
Warneton
Lys River
La Basse Ville
loegsteert Wood
0
2000
4000 metres
Front-line, morning, 6 June 1917
Evening, 7 June 1917
Evening, 31 July 1917
Morning, 20 September 1917
4–12 October 1917

CHAPTER EIGHT

MESSINES, 1917

A trench,
A stench,
Some scraps of French
Some horrible German vapours.
A shell,
A yell,
No more to tell,
Bar a paragraph in the papers.

ANONYMOUS

THE YPRES SALIENT in Flanders, Belgium, was already well known to the Australians and New Zealanders. Since the start of the war, the British had fought desperately to hold Ypres—the battered town was now a symbol of British resistance.

Seven to eight kilometres in front of Ypres, a low, sickle-shaped chain of hills, rising sharply at Messines, curved for 32 kilometres around Ypres before petering out into long spurs. The Germans had held the ridges and spurs since 1915, after using gas against the British. On these heights were the towns of Broodseinde and Passchendaele, the gaunt, shattered stumps of Polygon Wood, and Menin Road—names which now spoke of famous battles and bloodshed. From the heights, the Germans observed Ypres and the low, destroyed farmland in front of the town, and shelled anything that moved or could be used for observation. It was one of the deadliest and most heavily shelled areas on the Western Front. In 25 square kilometres, hundreds of thousands of men had already been killed.

With the French Army in disarray and unable to take part in joint offensives, Field Marshal Haig returned to his plan to attack in Flanders. He wanted to push the Germans off the heights surrounding Ypres, believing they would sacrifice division after division to hold them. The British War Council was reluctant after the heavy casualties of the Somme but agreed to his plan.

Before the Germans could be forced from the Ypres heights, the lower ridgeline ending at the mediaeval town of

Messines had to be captured. General Sir Herbert Plumer, whose 2nd Army had been located in the area for two years, was a methodical and careful planner. He favoured a new step-by-step method of fighting, in which the troops would not advance beyond the range of their artillery. Over the previous two years, he had also overseen the digging of 21 tunnels under the German lines, which, packed with explosives, would be detonated just before zero hour on the day of the planned offensive, 7 June.

After the explosions, three British corps were to advance to capture the ridge. The II Anzac Corps, which had been reorganised to include the New Zealand Division, the 25th British Division and the 3rd Australian Division, would be on the far-right flank below Messines. All three divisions would advance beyond Messines village, which the New Zealanders were to capture, and dig in just beyond the crest of the ridge. Then the 4th Australian Division, on loan to the corps, was to capture the second German defences—the Oosttaverne Line—1600 metres on, once the artillery had softened them. Many of the 4th Division felt they hadn't had long enough to rest after Bullecourt. It was to be the 3rd Division's first battle. Commanded by General John Monash, the men had arrived from England in November 1916 and were nicknamed 'Dinks', after the saying 'fair dinkum'. They hadn't signed up during the high spirits at the outbreak of the war but afterwards, knowing it was going to be a long and hard campaign.

From the end of April, the Australians and New Zealanders camped in Ploegsteert Wood. In front of them, perched at the top of a steep hill, was Messines. As the offensive drew closer, the men inspected a miniature model of what they were expected to capture, complete with farms, streams and villages. Below them, battles raged between Australian and German miners.

The Australian miners were tasked with defending two of the 21 tunnels that had been excavated through the deep blue clay. In the stale air, they dug in search of German miners who, themselves, were digging to find the tunnels. If distant thudding was heard, the Australians tunnelled cautiously towards it, checking to see if the mice or canaries they used to detect dangerous gases were still alive. When they got close, a listener waited alone. If the Germans were digging towards the main tunnels, the Australians detonated explosives against the wall, caving in the shafts.

For seven months the Australians dug and fought in the mines, trapping and killing Germans, as well as being buried and killed by them. One detonation trapped Sapper Edward Earl, who continued listening to German movement, wrote to his mother, wrote his will, then slept on and off for two days until rescued. He later died because of his time underground, but he and the other miners had kept the tunnels safe for the upcoming battle.

THE BATTLE OF MESSINES

By June, Messines was in ruins, its green slope churned and upturned. The Allied artillery had shelled all approaches to the village, and the Germans, cut off, hunkered in dugouts—some three to four storeys deep with stairs on either side leading up to the trenches. They were exhausted from the constant explosions and the effort of breathing through gasmasks. Unexpectedly, the safety of their shelters sapped the German troops of courage: the thumping shells and the shaking land made it increasingly difficult for the men to leave the dugouts.

On the dark night of 6 June, the 3rd Division, New Zealand and British troops marched towards the jumping-off point. They passed the artillery lined up wheel to wheel. As each gun fired, the flash from its muzzle threw an eerie light over the trees and gunners. Beforehand, some of the men had listened to their padre praying, then had sung hymns. Now, they heard the soft patter of the German Phosgene gas shells.

With horses and mules gasping in the poisonous air, each man put on his gasmask, squeezed the clips onto his nose to block his nostrils, then breathed out hard through a rubber tube and in through chemical-soaked fabric which neutralised the gas. All too quickly the glass eye-pieces fogged up and they struggled to breathe or see clearly as they walked on. Those who hadn't got their masks on in time gasped for breath, retched, vomited and collapsed, frothing from the mouth. The others eventually stumbled out of the gas clouds, pulled off their masks to suck in fresh air, then lay down at the jumping-off point.

The moon shone brightly. A British aeroplane flew over to drown out the noise of advancing tanks. Ten minutes before zero hour, the officers ordered their men to silently fix bayonets. At 3.05 a.m., five minutes before zero hour, German star flares shot up and several New Zealand machine guns opened fire. The Australians wondered if the attack had been detected before it had begun, but just before zero hour, all was silent again. Then 19 of the 21 mines exploded under the German lines.

Some of the Australians and New Zealanders were knocked over by the force of the blast. Black earth and flames, German troops and concrete blockhouses were heaved into the air. All along the line, British, Australian and New Zealand troops charged up the dust-shrouded slope. The apprehension and fear the men felt leading up to zero hour were now gone. For Lance Corporal Robert Bett, it was nothing to stop and bandage a mate's bad wound or to notice 'men killed alongside you, even when you get their blood spilt on you'. One New Zealander, Private Len Coley, stopped to cut off the mangled leg of a comrade and tried to carry him back but, even with a tourniquet, the man soon died from loss of blood. German SOS rockets burst into two green stars but the answering shells fell behind the rapidly advancing troops.

The first German trench was crowded with wire, broken timber, concrete and dirt, and, as the barrage left it, the Australians and New Zealanders swept in. German dead lay everywhere and the survivors seemed too stunned to fight. They emerged with their hands raised, shouting '*Kamerad*'—comrade. Within 16 minutes, the first trench had been taken, and as demoralised prisoners were sent back to prison cages, fresh troops followed the creeping barrage up the slope.

At the edge of the village, German machine-gunners kept firing in spite of the British artillery barrage. Lance Corporal Samuel Frickleton led a group of men through the exploding shells and bombed then bayoneted the crew of the nearest gun. He then attacked a second gun, killing its three gunners and nine others who refused to leave their dugout. He was one of 10 New Zealanders to be awarded the Victoria Cross at the Western Front.

With the nearest machine guns out of action, the New Zealanders waited below the heavily fortified ruins of Messines. Each man had a map of the village that indicated the positions of fortified cellars and five concrete shelters, which gave the Germans a perfect line of fire down the main streets. As the barrage crept through the village, the New Zealanders moved into the dust-swirling streets, fighting from cellar to cellar and from strong point to strong point. Many German gunners kept firing right to the last second, then surrendered. When they emerged with their hands up, revenge crossed the minds of many troops, especially after seeing their friends die around them. 'It's our turn,' Bett later wrote, 'you have to decide, shall I kill.' Some New Zealanders shot or bayoneted the surrendering Germans, but Bett saw them as 'poor, frightened devils', so demoralised they didn't even need an armed escort to take them to the wire cages.

With the sun rising, the Australians and British on either side of Messines advanced, joined by two fresh New Zealand battalions that had passed around the town. Following dust clouds raised by the creeping barrage, and under sniper fire, they pressed on, clearing heavily defended shell holes and rushing farm ruins. The Australians were shot down by gunners who'd left their dugouts and lined the hedges of a broken farm. Private Matthew Gray, a miner from New South Wales, crept up to the hedge and spotted two Germans at the gun—the rest of their crew lay dead around them. When Gray shot one of them, the other surrendered. The farm was finally taken after another crew was killed by 16-year-old Private Henry 'Glen' Sternbeck, who'd enlisted under another name when he was 15. By 5.20 a.m., pigeons returned to headquarters with news that the Australian, New Zealand and British troops were digging in.

THE PILLBOXES OF OOSTTAVERNE

Concealed by a cloud of dust spewed up by the barrage, the British, Australians and New Zealanders dug new trenches as British pilots shot down enemy aeroplanes attempting to locate the new lines. The 4th Australian Division moved up the Messines slope, with horse-drawn artillery racing ahead to new positions for the next advance. In the mid-afternoon, they set out to capture the Oosttaverne Line.

Twelve hours had passed since the start of the battle, and the recovering Germans waited in their blockhouses—nick-named pillboxes. Built above ground out of solid concrete, each pillbox was fortified and positioned to give covering fire to the troops—only a direct hit by the heaviest of artillery shells could damage them. As soon as the barrage had passed, the German gunners fired through loopholes in the concrete, while others poured out to shoot from the cover of dense hedges and trenches.

It was the first time the Australians had encountered pillboxes but they adapted quickly, creeping forward to get behind them, while Lewis gunners fired at the loopholes, their bullets splintering concrete into the Germans' faces. It was slow and fierce and the Germans showed no sign of surrendering. Captain Robert Grieve and his men hid in a shell hole under machine-gun fire from a pillbox. Beside Grieve, two soldiers tried to repair their machine gun with wire from the entanglements, but when the gun was hit again, Grieve grabbed a bag of bombs and hurled them, one after the other, scrambling forward under the cover of the explosions until he was past the firing line of the machine gun. Crawling under the loophole, he threw in several bombs, killing the gun crew. At another pillbox, soldiers had got behind it and fired into the back entrance until the screams and whimpers ceased.

With the nearest pillboxes captured, the 4th Division stacked the dead outside and used the blockhouses as headquarters, first-aid posts or resting places, while the dead men's skin blackened under the hot sun. Only one part of the line hadn't been captured, and, as the men dug in, German machine-gunners fired in the distance. The Australians launched several more futile charges. In one, Lieutenant Thomas McIntyre knew he couldn't fulfil his orders to capture a pillbox—it hadn't been hit by a single shell. All he said was, 'Alright Sir, if it is to be taken it will be taken.' When he led his men over the top, he was killed alongside them.

Several days later, the Germans withdrew. Over 7500 men had been taken prisoner and all objectives captured. The battle had been so successful that many troops wanted to push on and capture the German guns that began shelling the new Allied trenches, but Plumer preferred small advances, to prevent the troops becoming too exhausted to defend their position.

Within 48 hours, long mule trains were transporting hot food and tea up to yet another front-line trench the men had dug. With so much digging in, the New Zealanders and Australians were now referring to themselves as 'Diggers'.

HUMAN LIKE US

Before burying the dead, the men searched them for letters to loved ones, diaries, or other things of value to be sent home. They also hunted through German pockets for letters and photos either to keep as souvenirs or so they could be returned to the soldier's family. Lance Corporal Bett felt that

> Somehow we get wrong ideas, we forget the Hun is human like us, has his home, his loved ones and sweethearts, and it was pathetic to look through the

> private belongings of the Huns we buried, and see his photos, and little Bible and treasures.

To many Australians and New Zealanders, the German was a 'Boche', a 'Hun', a 'Fritz', an enemy they rarely saw—it was 'old Fritz' that sent over shells or fired SOS rockets or was shot. The Diggers were eager to punish them for starting the war and for the atrocities they'd committed. They wanted, as Captain Harold Armitage wrote, to 'make our names stand out in Hunnish blood'. Some wanted nothing more than to use their bayonets on them. When Private David Harford first killed a German

> a queer thrill shot through me, it was a different feeling to that which I had when I shot my first Kangaroo when I was a boy. For an instant I felt sick and faint, but the feeling soon passed; and I was normal and looking for more shots.

Similarly, Sergeant Eric Evans 'felt little emotion, just intense excitement'. Even after battles, men itched 'for another smack at the rotten Hun'.

Time allowed some soldiers to reflect on their actions and their beliefs about the 'enemy'. Second Lieutenant Simon Fraser recalled how everyone cheered when their artillery smashed in German trenches,

> but one does not think till afterwards that some poor devils may be flying up with it, who are just as anxious for the war to end as we are.

Private John Wright came to see them as ordinary men, like himself: 'I don't think old Fritz is any better or worse than

New Zealand troops training for an attack on Messines, Belgium.
Alexander Turnbull Library G- 12753-1/2

our soldiers.' And when Evans saw a mixture of German and Allied dead, he felt that it no longer mattered which side they were on. 'They are dead, and for their loved ones, that is all that matters.'

Like the Australians and New Zealanders, the Germans volunteered to defend their country and for adventure. One soldier, 19-year-old Ernst Jünger, volunteered on the first day of the war and marched out 'in a rain of flowers' from well-wishers. After growing up 'in an age of security, we shared a yearning for danger...We thought of it as manly...Anything to participate, not to have to stay at home.'

In the trenches, the Germans faced the same conditions as the Allies. They stamped their feet for warmth, used helmets as basins to wash in and, when it was quiet, thought of home. They too grew quiet as they marched forward through shell storms. They buried and mourned their dead and accepted cigarettes and bars of chocolate offered to them by captured soldiers. From craters, they watched and listened to low-flying aeroplanes circling 'vulture-like' overhead, emitting 'a series of low long-drawn-out siren tones' to alert their artillery. More often than not, shells would follow. During battles the men knew that if they fell, they'd be left to die—a fellow soldier told Jünger that 'No one can help... Everyone knows this is about life or death.'

THE SOUR SMELL OF NEW DEATH

Within days, the New Zealanders and the 3rd Division began patrolling closer to the Warneton Line, the third line of German defence that had become the Germans' new frontline. In the dark, they bombed fortified strong points set up in farm ruins and craters. At dawn, the front-line troops returned to newly set up posts in shell holes and pulled over camouflage netting to prevent aeroplanes from finding them. It was dangerous work, and the German machine-gunners were active. New Zealander Private Sidney 'Stan' Stanfield saw his mate Private James Hallett, a shepherd from Waipukurau, get shot as they moved out of a trench. He recalled when he returned the following day to bury him,

> poor old Jim was laying there, cuddled up in a heap,

> as men die. Don't forget we were all young, we didn't die easy. You don't die at once, you're not shot and killed stone dead. We were fit and highly trained, and of course we didn't die easy. You were slow to die, and you'd find them huddled up in a heap like kids gone to sleep, you know; cuddled up dead.

It had been hoped that the Germans would withdraw, but instead they strengthened their posts as their artillery tore into the Allied trenches and gassed and bombed the areas behind. Lieutenant George Mitchell saw a single shell kill seven men, leaving only shattered remains. The air stank of hot blood: 'the sour smell of new death, mingled with the hated acid of high explosive.' From a distance, machine-gunners fired at the men. An Australian officer who was new to the line asked Mitchell to knock out a troublesome machine gun, saying, 'You've got a decoration. How about you going out and silencing it?' Mitchell replied, after some thought, 'How about you going out and capturing it. Then you'll have a decoration too.' Neither went out.

Where possible, the men slept in the safety of captured German dugouts and pillboxes. With each close shell-burst the pillboxes would ring and rock. At times, only the 'occasional cry of "Stretcher-bearers!" broke the horrific monotony of whirring and crashing shells'.

In July, Mitchell was woken by a series of shell explosions. Then the daylight streaming into the entrance was blocked by his skipper, stumbling down the stairs, saying, 'I'm hit.' His voice filled Mitchell with a 'dragging, cold dread'. The officer had been trying to move men to safety when a tiny piece of shrapnel had pierced his chest. With each pulse, blood spurted from the wound. The officer, knowing he was dying, kept saying 'I'm done, I'm done.' Mitchell knew he couldn't help him but he still tried to stem the blood. Tears fell down his face. There was nothing he could say to comfort him. Blood gurgled into the officer's chest. 'Say good-bye to the boys. Tell my wife—' he started, before saying a prayer.

After the officer died, Mitchell climbed back into bed and slept. It was all he could do. It was what he had to do to survive at the front.

KILLED IN ACTION

CAPTAIN HAROLD ARMITAGE
School teacher. 3 April 1917

SECOND LIEUTENANT SIMON FRASER
Farmer. 11 May 1917

PRIVATE JAMES HALLETT
Shepherd. 8 June 1917

LIEUTENANT THOMAS MCINTYRE
Carpenter. 10 June 1917

PRIVATE MATTHEW GRAY
Miner. 12 October 1917

DIED OF WOUNDS

PRIVATE DAVID HARFORD
Miner. 31 March 1917

LANCE CORPORAL ROBERT BETT
Coachbuilder. 15 June 1917

SAPPER EDWARD EARL
Labourer. 28 July 1917

CHAPTER NINE

THIRD BATTLE OF YPRES, 1917

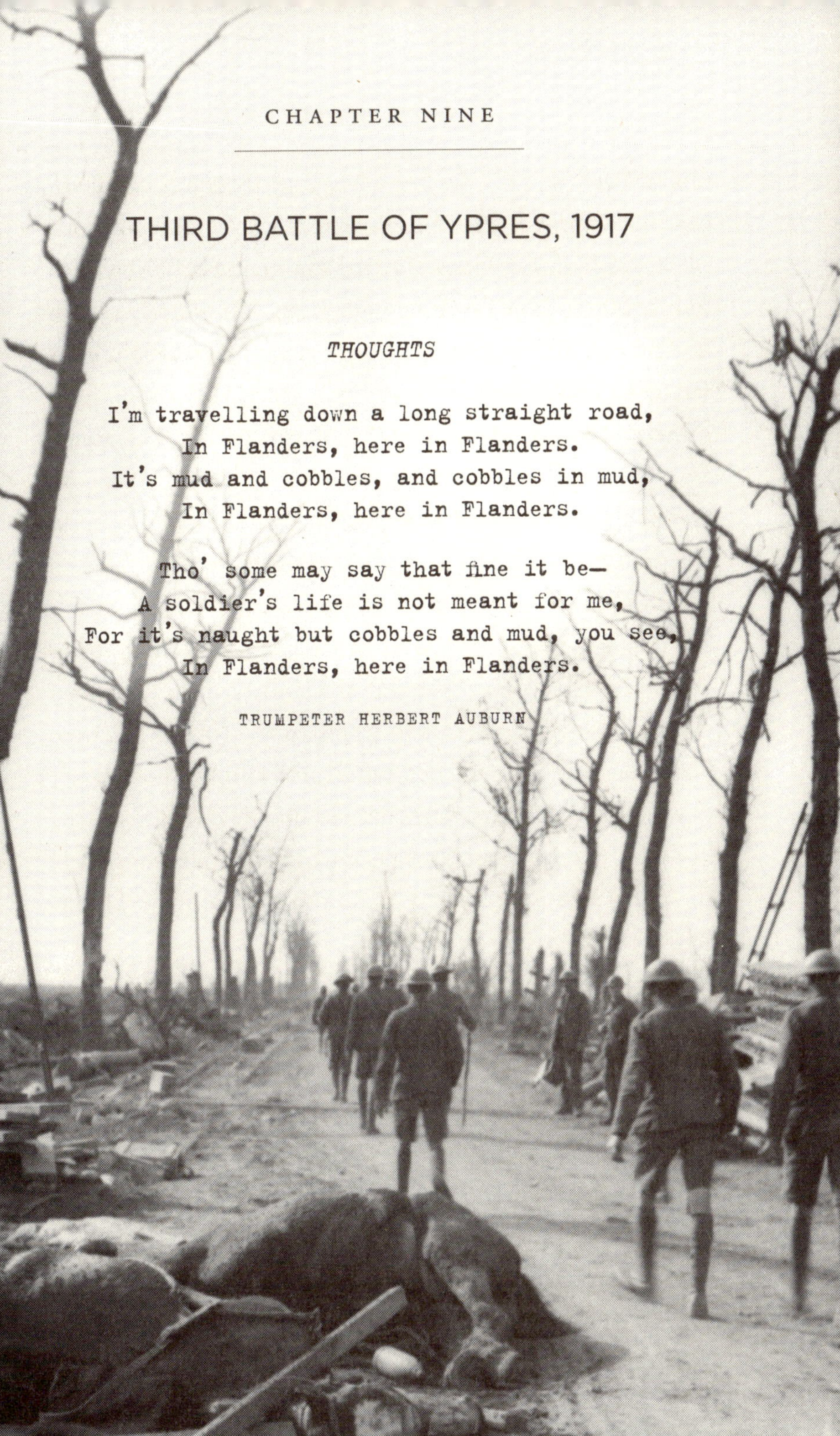

THOUGHTS

I'm travelling down a long straight road,
In Flanders, here in Flanders.
It's mud and cobbles, and cobbles in mud,
In Flanders, here in Flanders.

Tho' some may say that fine it be—
A soldier's life is not meant for me,
For it's naught but cobbles and mud, you see,
In Flanders, here in Flanders.

TRUMPETER HERBERT AUBURN

ON 22 JULY, with the lower Messines ridgeline captured, over 3000 British guns began saturating the Ypres heights in preparation for Field Marshal Haig's main offensive to force the Germans from the high ground. Through a series of advances, British troops were to extend the line eight kilometres to Passchendaele.

To create a diversion, II Anzac Corps prepared to attack the Warneton Line, 10 kilometres from Ypres, but the Germans, watching the preparations from the heights, knew where the real advance was going to come from.

On 31 July, the first advance began—to Pilckem Ridge—but the right flank of the British troops' 27-kilometre front was stopped at Menin Road by machine-gun fire between the shattered remains of two woodlands—Inverness Copse and Glencorse Wood. Then rain began falling: the heaviest downpour in 75 years. The complex drainage systems of the low-lying Flanders area had been destroyed by the war, and the rains quickly turned the land into a sea of mud. Orders were given to halt the attack.

Two hours after the British advanced, II Anzac Corps attacked the Warneton Line. Two battalions of the 3rd Division charged outposts while the New Zealanders fought from house to house in La Basse Ville. Then the rain blew in from Ypres.

The battlefield from La Basse Ville to Ypres became a bog. Men stood with their backs to trench walls, coats sodden and filthy, their wet socks and boots sinking into the mud.

HOPE DRIES UP

In the following weeks, further attacks over the churned mud and flooded craters failed to seize the woods. By the end of August the British held only the edge of Inverness Copse—through harsh fighting it had changed hands 18 times. Haig, who'd believed that the Germans were demoralised, had abandoned General Plumer's small advances in favour of deeper ones, but now it was British morale that was suffering. One captured British soldier said he'd gladly shoot the officers who'd ordered the attacks.

Haig was determined to continue so, with Plumer in charge, a new offensive beginning on 20 September was planned to capture the centre of the Ypres heights. The area around Menin Road and the two woods was the first objective—an advance of 1300 metres in three short stages—then, further along the ridge, Polygon Wood and Broodseinde. From there, two more advances would see Passchendaele captured and the German line possibly broken. With the British divisions exhausted, the 1st, 2nd and 5th Australian Divisions of I Anzac Corps moved to Ypres after a long period of resting and training. The 4th Australian Division, which had fought with II Anzac Corps at Messines, was also back with the corps.

MENIN ROAD

In the darkness of 20 September, the 1st and 2nd Divisions, fighting side by side for the first time, huddled close to Inverness Copse and Glencorse Wood. Once leafy and beautiful, the woods were now black and skeletal against the skyline. The men were on the southern part of the ridge, and to their right was Menin Road, which ran from Ypres to Menin. Flares revealed shadowy pillboxes in the distance. Zero hour, 5.40 a.m., was close. The Australians readied themselves, then, with British divisions on either side, they advanced.

For five days, the artillery had bombarded the now-dry land with 1.5 million shells. It had crushed the fighting spirit of the Germans; many emerged from pillboxes waving white cloths as the Australians charged. The first and second stages fell quickly, and with the shattered woods in their hands, the men waited in captured pillboxes or shell holes, eating sandwiches, smoking German cigars and even reading newspapers.

One Australian group in a pillbox was surprised by a German messenger dog. In a metal tube tied to its neck was an order for the men who should have been in the pillbox to immediately recapture the lost land. But they were dead, wounded or prisoners helping to stretcher out the wounded. Their comrades further back were then expected to retake the land, but they had to advance through a storm of shells and no counterattack reached the Australians.

At the end of the third stage, the troops dug in as shells exploded around them. The men were in high spirits: the attack had been quick, limited and successful across the 12-kilometre front. They were relieved from the front-line that night.

Still, over 5000 Australians had been killed or wounded,

most as they dug in. In this battle, as in others, families lost more than one son or brother. The Seabrook family of Five Dock in Sydney received three telegrams afterwards, one for each son that fought beside Menin Road. Theo was 25, George, 24 and William, 21. It had been their first battle. The bodies of Theo and George were never found. William, who was mortally wounded and died the following day, was buried nearby. It was devastating news for their parents and their youngest brother would never speak about it in his lifetime.

POLYGON WOOD

Over the next six days, soldiers worked through shellfire and mustard gas—a new German gas that burned and blistered the skin—to build new roads so the artillery could be moved forward to support the next advance. At dusk, 80 motor lorries dumped road planks near the deadly Hellfire Corner for horse-drawn carts to transport to the next section of road being built. Menin Road, and particularly the railway crossing at Hellfire Corner, were shelled regularly, so transports raced through to avoid random shells. At Hellfire Corner, screens of cloth shielded moving troops and wagons from observation. With shells exploding around them, cart drivers steadied their horses, while soldiers dragged dead horses and smashed wagons from the road.

On 26 September, with the artillery in position, the 4th and 5th Divisions lay at the jumping-off line, facing the thin, shattered stumps of Polygon Wood as German flares lit up the night. In the centre of seven divisions on a nine-kilometre front, the Diggers were again to advance 1300 metres in three steps, their objective to capture the wood. At 5.50 a.m., the British artillery barrage intensified, spewing up walls of dust and smoke as it rolled forward 'like a Gippsland bushfire'. While many Germans fought as determinedly as in the past, others were stunned and disorientated by the heavy bombardment. When the barrage passed over, many surrendered to the advancing Australians. Some even held out souvenirs for their captors. 'Old Fritz's morale vanishes when he knows we are coming,' said Sergeant Eric Evans.

As British biplanes flew overhead to locate the new front-line, the Australians sheltered in shell holes and lit fires to brew tea. Reinforcements helped dig the new front-line under fire, only stopping to take souvenirs from passing German prisoners. Evans used several prisoners as stretcher-bearers: 'It's great sport, driving them on at revolver point.'

The Germans were demoralised; they'd either held the front-line under crushing bombardments or counter-attacked through withering shellfire. The Australians and British were feeling more positive; the short attacks on wide fronts after proper preparation were succeeding. In front of them lay Broodseinde Ridge, abandoned by the British in 1915 and now crowded with German headquarters and observation posts.

Since 7 June, the Allies had captured three-quarters of the sickle-shaped ridge. The next advance was to see Broodseinde Ridge captured, then, after that, Passchendaele.

Hellfire Corner on the Menin Road, in the Ypres sector. AWM E01889

New Zealand soldiers passing the ruins of the Cloth Hall in Ypres.
Alexander Turnbull Library, G- 13129-1/2

SHOCK TROOPS

On 28 September, after a period of resting and training 70 kilometres away, the New Zealand and 3rd Australian Divisions—II Anzac Corps—marched through Ypres, passing the ruins of the ancient Cloth Hall. Hooves and iron wheels clattered and clanged over the cobbled roads as they moved out through Menin Gate towards the front-line. The move had been rushed and the marches to Ypres long and hard—the next advance had been brought forward as the commanders feared that the good weather might end.

The air carried the smell of death. Duckboard tracks wove around a cratered, devastated land dotted with captured pillboxes, ruined tanks, and dead, bloated horses and mules. Villages were mounds of rubble and streams were bogs. Cemeteries were the only thing growing. Some graves had crosses inscribed 'Rest in Peace' or '*Hier ruht in Gott*'—here rests in God. Others were simply marked by an upturned rifle with a helmet on top. To Lieutenant Colonel Claud Weston, 'every square yard of it seemed foul with slaughter.'

The Australians and New Zealanders joined the front-line at night. Both the British command and the Germans now considered them shock troops or storm troops: soldiers who could be given the role of taking the hardest and most vital areas. Evans felt it was deserved: 'We are given a damn lot of work in every hopover and we have earnt the name of "shock troops" from our enemies.' The II Anzac Corps hadn't suffered a defeat at the Western Front yet, and their morale was high after Messines. Private Stan Stanfield came to believe that this self-confidence was misguided:

> Of course don't forget the propaganda—we were brainwashed that we were so good that you had to be good. We were taught not to lay down, therefore we didn't lay down.

The battle for Broodseinde Ridge was to be launched on 4 October, on a 12-kilometre front with 12 divisions. The Australians and New Zealanders were on the right flank of the advance. From left to right, the New Zealanders and the 3rd Division were to seize Gravenstafel Spur, while the 1st and 2nd Divisions were to capture Broodseinde village. This would leave only the northern part of the ridge, including Passchendaele, for the next advances. For the first time, three Australian divisions and the New Zealand Division would fight beside each other, and each was keen to prove itself better than the others. According to Australian Sergeant Henry Kahan, 'We always believed we were the best and the New Zealanders second best and there were times when I privately reversed that order but I didn't say so publicly.'

Striking differences had developed between the New Zealanders and the Australians. The New Zealanders were more disciplined, neater, and they were quieter, less likely to sing or be raucous when marching or on leave. Once, while a group of New Zealanders were resting in a canteen, several Australians walked in and immediately sat down at the piano and broke into song. After they left, one of the New Zealanders complained about how 'doleful' his own countrymen were. Why couldn't they 'pipe up like the Aussies'? he wondered. But when asked why he didn't join the singalong himself, he answered, 'The trouble is I'm a New Zealander.' The New Zealanders were seen as 'stern, dour and grim' and became known as the Silent Division.

BROODSEINDE

On 4 October, the divisions of the Anzac corps waited in small coffin-like holes or fortified shell holes, hoping the weather would hold. Flares crackled yellow through the hazy drizzle. It was a freezing night, and, as zero hour approached, the men sheltered under waterproof sheets, occasionally stretching their numb, cramped legs. At 5.40 a.m., 40 minutes before zero hour, they heard the familiar 'crump, crump' of German artillery. The shells hit the Australians hard. By dawn, their dead littered the churned-up land—one in seven men had been killed or wounded. Australian Major Philip Howell-Price had been removed from his battalion to spare his life after his two brothers were killed, one at Flers, the other at Bullecourt, but he'd chosen to return when he heard they were attacking. He was never seen again. Officers were uncertain if their men could still attack at zero hour, but when the British barrage began, the Australians shook themselves out of their shell holes, some lighting cigarettes as they crossed the wet ground behind a deafening barrage that hissed up steam and mud rather than a blanket of dust.

The enemy shelling had been part of a planned counterattack to win back ground, and as the Australians advanced, they met a line of advancing Germans. The Australian riflemen and Lewis gunners shot as they walked, breaking the German attack.

Beside the Australians, the New Zealanders found hundreds of German dead scattered among craters, caught out in the open by a barrage so loud that soldiers struggled to hear the man next to them even if he was shouting. After recent battles, the Germans were holding their front-line heavily in order to stop attacks immediately, rather than sending reinforcements from their support lines. Now their front-line troops were trapped between the Diggers and the barrage that had passed behind them.

Machine-gunners fired desperately from the pillboxes. One German officer, revolver in hand, led his men out to charge the New Zealanders. All the Germans were shot down. New officers replaced the fallen as each pillbox was outflanked and bombed. By 9.30 a.m., the Anzac corps were digging in at their final objectives, 1700 metres from where they had started. Broodseinde Ridge, the village and Gravenstafel Spur had been captured.

The Diggers lit red flares to indicate their positions, then covered their new shell-hole posts in camouflage netting. One and a half kilometres along the tip of the sickle-shaped ridge was the red-roofed village of Passchendaele. The New Zealanders, who were on the forward slope of Gravenstafel Spur, looked across a bogged valley at Bellevue Spur, which joined Passchendaele Ridge. Pillboxes lay stark on the spur and gunners fired freely from them, their bullets sweeping no-man's-land.

With over 5000 Germans surrendering, their few remaining soldiers had only just managed to plug the gaps. Waves of German troops tried to counterattack but were shot down. Officers on horseback tried to round up and rally their scattering troops for another charge, but every time a shell landed among them, the troops fled.

The Germans were disorganised and their commanders seemed powerless to stop the Allied advances. In 15 days, the Allies had struck successfully three times. Many of the officers and troops had wanted to keep advancing and most now believed that if the weather held, the Germans could be forced off the heights. The Germans were exhausted. Many of those surrendering were young—17- or 18-year-olds—and quick to thank their captors. The German commander of the area, Crown Prince Rupprecht of Bavaria, was considering withdrawing from the ridge.

With victory in sight, Field Marshal Haig rushed General Plumer's step-by-step tactics and ordered the next advance for 9 October, in five day's time, leaving little time for the artillery to do its job effectively. At noon, rain fell. The Diggers helped their wounded, placing oil sheets over them to keep the rain off, lighting their cigarettes, giving them water or carrying them to crowded pillboxes converted into aid posts.

All Black legend Sergeant Dave Gallaher had been shot in the throat and, like other wounded, he lay outdoors while rain lashed and shells exploded around him. He died later that day. New Zealander Private Robin Hamley had been shot in the neck and stomach. While waiting, he wrote in his diary,

> Dear M, D and G
> Think I'm dying
> Best love
> don't fret
> Tell Dorothy
> Rob.

He died two days later.

In the trenches the surviving soldiers leaned against the wall because there was no dry place to sit. They were soaked and smeared in stinking Flanders mud. New Zealander Private Neil Ingram spoke for many when he said he would prefer 'a pig's life, humans were not made for this.' The following day, rations arrived. The biscuits were flecked with the blood of horses and men killed while bringing them up. When the men were relieved later that night, Ingram and those left in his company ate a feast of hot stew. The cooks had prepared food for 120 but only 30 men were still standing. When mail arrived for the dead, Ingram and the other survivors opened it and shared out the knitted clothing and food.

DRY AS A BONE, POELCAPPELLE

On the night of 5 October, the 49th and 66th British Divisions followed signposts through the featureless landscape to the front-line. They had been loaned to Lieutenant General Godley's II Anzac Corps for the next attack. Their advance was one of two steps. They were to advance the line to the outskirts of Passchendaele, supported by the 2nd Australian Division. Then on 12 October, the 3rd Australian and the New Zealand Divisions were to go on to capture the long-sought-after village. The attack should have been postponed—the weather hampered the preparations essential for the step-by-step tactics, and the bogged land and roads had prevented most of the artillery getting into position. Haig, convinced that the German Army was close to collapse, believed too much had been gained to stop now. But rain was still falling.

On 7 October, Haig held a conference with the local commanders to determine whether the attack could still be carried out, stressing 'that there should be no postponement unless absolutely necessary'. In a conference with war correspondents, one general said the attack should proceed even if the weather was bad—the valleys might be muddy but the ridge itself was 'as dry as a bone'. After the conference, one correspondent commented:

> The official attitude is that Passchendaele Ridge is so important that to-morrow's attack is worth making whether it succeeds or fails...I suspect that they are making a great, bloody experiment—a huge gamble...I feel, and most of the correspondents feel...terribly anxious.

Lieutenant General Birdwood, commander of I Anzac Corps, also hoped the advance would be postponed, but, as the 2nd Division only had a minor role on the British flank, he kept quiet.

The attack went ahead on 9 October at 5.20 a.m., with the troops already exhausted from an 11-hour march to the front-line. Against a feeble resistance, and with large numbers of Germans surrendering, soldiers from the 66th Division made it to the village outskirts, but the 49th Division made no progress up the Bellevue Spur. German gunners shot them down, then turned their guns onto the 66th Division, which was forced to retreat, ending up just 450 metres from where they had started. The 2nd Division, which was supporting the 66th's flank, was also forced back down the slope.

By dusk, the attack was over. The 66th Division was reported as being just short of the first objective. It was therefore decided, possibly on the advice of Godley, that enough ground had been gained for a sufficient jumping-off position to seize Passchendaele village. Godley hadn't visited the front-line; nor had Major General Monash or Major General Russell.

Haig ordered the next advance to take place in three days' time. He had to secure the heights—failing to do so would mean that all who'd died over the previous 10 weeks had died for nothing. Blinded by Passchendaele Ridge, Haig told journalists that it was Flanders mud that had defeated the last attack, not the German Army. He said the Germans were at breaking point, and, despite the mud, all that stood between the Australians and the New Zealanders and success were 'flesh and blood...not blockhouses. They take a month to make.'

Haig's staff should have informed him of the conditions, but they didn't. He should have known that the attacks, like those in the August rain, would fail. Even if the British divisions were at the first objective, the Australians and New Zealanders still had to advance 2300 metres: the New Zealanders to capture Bellevue Spur; the 3rd Division, Passchendaele village, with one brigade of the 4th Division supporting its flank. They were to attempt what was initially meant to be two advances in one, a difficult task in dry conditions, let alone in the mud.

For the battle to succeed the artillery had to be in position, but with rain still falling, the guns became bogged. The gunners laid debris under the wheels for traction, and, when the horses sank up to their bellies in the mud, long lines of 100 men dragged the guns forward. But few made it to their new positions and those that did sank and shifted with every shot. The guns couldn't be fired accurately. The gunners, sick from sleeping in sodden dugouts, were now expected to increase their rate of fire to make up for the lack of guns, but there weren't enough shells: the pack mules bringing them up were floundering. Some fell into boggy shell holes, disappearing altogether or needing their handlers' help to keep their heads above the surface. Those that couldn't be pulled out had to be shot. It now took 17 hours instead of one to reach the front-line, and each shell that arrived had to be cleaned of mud before being fired. When the Diggers took over from the British in the early hours of 11 October, the pillboxes and wire on Bellevue Spur stood brutally intact.

FIRST BATTLE OF PASSCHENDAELE

The front-line was littered with dead and wounded from the 49th and 66th British Divisions. 'Stretcher bearer,' they called, and, 'For God's sake come here.' Australian Lieutenant Walde Fisher arrived at 'one pillbox to find it just a mass of dead'. At the next one, he found

> about fifty men alive...Never have I seen men so broken or demoralised. They were huddled up close

> behind the box in the last stages of exhaustion and fear.

When daylight arrived, the Australians and New Zealanders crept out and moved from one waterlogged crater to the next to give the wounded food or water. If they could, they carried them back to crowded first-aid posts. All through the grey, bleak afternoon, stretcher-bearers worked to carry men out. Private Leonard Hart was dumbfounded that the British officers had abandoned the wounded: 'I have seen some pretty rotten sights during the two and a half years of active service, but I must say that this fairly sickened me.'

At the same time, the II Anzac Corps commanders who had not visited the line were realising that the jumping-off point was practically the same as before the last attack. To offset the extra distance, the pace of the creeping barrage was doubled. Now the men would have to cross the first 450 metres in 20 minutes, a pace never attempted in dry weather, let alone in mud. According to Private Stanfield, the soldiers at Flanders were

> a pretty dumb beast. That's how he's treated, you see. He was only gun fodder, that's what I feel. We were pretty dumb beasts, or we wouldn't have been thrown into that sort of warfare, because it was hopeless before you started, we all knew that.

That night, as it rained heavily, the men moved to their jumping-off positions, and by 4 a.m. they were waiting under waterproof sheets in shell holes for dawn and zero hour.

Opposite the New Zealanders was the blocked Ravebeek stream, muddy craters, wire entanglements, then the pillboxes on Bellevue Spur. The men hoped the artillery would destroy the wire, or that at least the pillboxes would be bombarded while they cut through it. But when the shelling eventuated, it was sporadic and brief. The Diggers wanted to do their best, but, as one New Zealand officer wrote in his diary:

> I do not feel as confident as usual. Things are being rushed too much. The weather is rotten, the roads very bad, and the objectives have not been properly bombarded. However, we will hope for the best.

Across no-man's-land, Crown Prince Rupprecht wrote in his diary: 'most gratifyingly—rain; our most effective ally'.

At 4.20 a.m. the rain stopped, but the wire in front was still intact. Then, at zero hour, 5.25 a.m., the men followed a creeping barrage of mud and steam, only to be shot down. Mud swallowed the dead and wounded and weighed the survivors down. They unclogged their guns and rifles and fired at the pillbox loopholes, momentarily forcing the Germans to take cover, while others slid forward to cut the wire. Second Lieutenants John Bishop and Norman Watson cut through both belts, then charged a pillbox. Short bursts from a machine gun killed them both before they could throw their bombs.

At 8 a.m., the New Zealanders were ordered to dig in and hold what little they'd gained of the slope. German gunners fired down at them from the spur as they dug into the sloppy mud. Around them, snipers hidden in trees, shell holes and even in the wire picked off men scurrying to find better shelter. Many of the men didn't see a single German that day.

Experiencing less opposition than the New Zealanders, the Australians of the 9th Brigade left a trail of dead and wounded as they outflanked pillboxes, then dug in at the second objective, 1900 metres from the start.

The 10th Brigade, next to the New Zealanders, hadn't got as far. With the New Zealanders out of action, the Germans on Bellevue Spur had turned their guns onto the advancing Australians. In groups of two or three, they scrambled from crater to crater, but with only 150 men remaining and just at their first objective, they dug in. While they waited for reinforcements, 20 of them set out for Passchendaele. They crept up a sheltered gully and walked straight into the village. There were no Germans, but there were no Australians in sight either, so the men returned to their comrades. With shells exploding around them, their officer, Major Lyndhurst Giblin, sent a message to headquarters asking 'What am I to do?' He'd already sent soldiers to suppress the fire from Bellevue Spur but they didn't return. At 3 p.m., orders were given to the Australians to withdraw to the starting point.

THE COLD TRUTH

The Australians and New Zealanders had failed. It was the New Zealanders' first defeat. Many blamed the commanders, particularly Lieutenant General Godley. One New

Zealander, Corporal Harold Green, believed 'the stunt should never have been ordered under such conditions. It was absolute murder.' Rifleman Henry Gibbens felt that the commanders—'the bloody heads'—should 'have been sent over the top instead of us. They had nothing ready and you were up to your hips in mud and water.'

That evening, with rain still falling, the men held on grimly to the little they'd gained. There were nearly 3000 New Zealand casualties, and more than 4000 Australian. The aid posts overflowed. Limbs hung from tendons; some men had huge holes in their bodies; and one shocked soldier continued to drink his coffee as it poured out of the bullet hole in his cheek. Doctors and orderlies toiled to help them but the wounded arrived faster than they could be seen to. Outside, men lay on the wet ground, shaking uncontrollably under 'cold driving rain and hail' and exploding shells.

Private George Tierney and five other stretcher-bearers struggled through the mud to carry out a wounded man but they soon had to stop: all were vomiting from the effects of an earlier gas attack. Around them, the walking wounded led other gas victims, their eyes bandaged over. With nothing left to vomit, Tierney retched continually as his eyes filled with water and swelled up. By the time he reached the hospital, he was blind. Nurses bathed his eyes and inserted cocaine under his eyelids before bandaging them, but 'the agony was awful…it was as though my eyes were full of sand.' The gas could cause lung-collapse and, over two nights, five men died. Tierney was kept alive by the hard work of New

Bringing supplies up through the mud, Ypres sector.
AWM E00963

Zealand nurses, who visited other hospitals on their days off to find New Zealand soldiers and see if they could help them. It took Tierney two weeks to regain his sight; others took much longer.

To cope with the numbers of wounded, extra battalions were sent forward to act as stretcher-bearers. It took eight men four hours to stretcher out a single soldier to advanced dressing stations, where doctors stitched up wounds, sawed off mangled limbs and applied splints to broken ones.

At the front-line, German soldiers held their fire and directed stretcher-bearers towards the wounded. But not all of them could be found. Men cried out at night. One kept calling over and over. Private Stanfield helped search for him but

> we couldn't find him and we heard him crying part of the next day. Calling, you know, calling, sort of crying, not screaming or anything, crying out. We just knew there was a wounded man lying down under something you see. We never found that man. That's the only thing that's stuck in my memory.

Twice now the Germans had defeated the Allies, and their spirits lifted. Their artillery fired over sneezing gas, which made it difficult to wear a mask, then mustard gas followed, blistering skin, swelling eyes and turning the men's voices hoarse. At night, Gotha bombers flew overhead, lit by the glare of British searchlights.

The Diggers were demoralised and depressed. Victory or defeat both came at a heavy cost. Men spoke of times before or after Passchendaele. They hated the war and could see no end to it. The thought of another winter filled them with despair.

A VICTORY TOO LATE

The Canadians took over and, at their commander's insistence, were given more time to prepare. They would seize in three advances what the Australians and New Zealanders had been expected to take in one. In bitter fighting, after an 11-day bombardment, they captured Bellevue Spur on 26 October, then Passchendaele on 10 November.

The Third Battle of Ypres finished three months after it had begun. Over 70,000 Allied soldiers had been killed and 200,000 wounded. Although the Germans lost fewer troops, their commanders worried they wouldn't recover from the damage done. They began to realise the war could be lost.

Then, on 20 November, 400 British tanks tore a 10-kilometre hole in the Hindenburg Line near Cambrai. It was a huge success—in one day the British gained six kilometres, over half what had been captured in the three-month Ypres offensive. People in Britain celebrated, and for the first time since the start of the war, church bells were rung in celebration. But 10 days later, the Germans counterattacked and regained the lost ground. Despite this victory, the German commanders knew they wouldn't survive if they continued to take a defensive approach to the war.

THE YEAR ENDS

The Australians stayed at Passchendaele for several more weeks, then all five divisions moved to Messines to rest and recover. For the first time since arriving on the Western Front, all the Australian divisions were together under one commander, Birdwood—now promoted to full general. The I Anzac Corps was renamed the Australian Corps, while II Anzac Corps became XXII Corps. The New Zealanders took over the line in front of Polygon Wood.

It was another hard winter. When the land froze, bullets ricocheted off the earth and fragments from exploding shells 'flew incredible distances'. Icicles hung from tin hats, and soldiers slipped on the duckboards. Gas lingered blue in the still air and the dead lay frozen and twisted.

The year ended, once again, in a stalemate. The German submarine campaign had not brought Britain to its knees; nor had the British driven the Germans from Belgium, although they had drawn German reserves away from the recovering French.

In Russia, troops sick of being poor, hungry and ill-treated, overthrew the tsar in a revolution and made peace with the Germans, but the peace treaty was a stark reminder of what the Allies were fighting for. In return for peace Russia gave Germany one-third of its agricultural land, half of its industry and most of its coalmines. With Russia out of the war, the Germans began moving their troops from the Eastern Front to the Western Front, exactly what Field Marshal Haig and others had feared. Over the following weeks, an extra 1000 guns and 35 divisions reached the front with the aim of attacking the Allies before the Americans arrived.

KILLED IN ACTION

PRIVATE GEORGE SEABROOK
Painter. 20 September 1917

PRIVATE THEO SEABROOK
Engine fireman. 20 September 1917

MAJOR PHILIP HOWELL-PRICE
Bank clerk. 4 October 1917

SECOND LIEUTENANT JOHN BISHOP
School teacher. 12 October 1917

SECOND LIEUTENANT NORMAN WATSON
12 October 1917

LIEUTENANT WALDE FISHER
Law student and tutor. 5 April 1918

DIED OF WOUNDS

SECOND LIEUTENANT WILLIAM SEABROOK
Telephonist. 21 September 1917

SERGEANT DAVE GALLAHER
Storeman. 4 October 1917

PRIVATE ROBIN HAMLEY
Schoolmaster. 6 October 1917

CHAPTER TEN

THE SPRING OFFENSIVE, 1918

BIRD—In loving memory of my dearly loved and only son, Pte. C. Bird (Charlie), 5th Batt., killed in action Mont St. Quentin, September 1, 1918.

I little thought when we said goodbye
We parted forever and you were to die.
We'll meet again, my dearest son.

INSERTED BY HIS LOVING MOTHER,
A. MADDEN.

NEWSPAPER 'IN MEMORIAM' NOTICE

ON 21 MARCH 1918, with thick fog hanging over the land, more than 6000 German guns opened fire across an 80-kilometre front at the Somme. For over five hours, their shells tore into the British trenches. Then German storm troops charged through the swirling mist. They carried their new light machine guns, bombs and entrenching tools, sharpened for hand-to-hand combat. After forcing gaps in the British line, they surged through them, leaving any heavily defended villages and strong points for following troops to capture. The resistance was, in places, more hardline than expected, and with no supplies the storm troops lived off food taken from British shelters—eating ham and bread and sucking raw eggs dry. They kept their water-cooled machine guns from overheating by filling the cooling system with urine.

The Spring Offensive was Germany's last attempt at a victory before the Americans arrived. Support for the war in Germany was weakening; there were strikes over food shortages, and the country was reaching the end of its manpower. Many wanted peace even if this meant handing back Belgium, but to the leaders and generals this was the same as losing the war. Instead, they attacked where the British and French Armies joined, with the aim of splitting them and driving the British back to the English Channel. Once the British were trapped and destroyed, the Germans believed the French would have little will to continue.

As the British were forced into retreat across the Somme, large gaps opened in the line, and ground that the Allies had captured in 1916 fell again—High Wood, Flers, Thiepval and Pozières. The British were in disarray, and large numbers of troops retreated in confusion as six massive German guns began shelling Paris.

GIVE A MAN A CHANCE

The New Zealand Division and the 3rd, 4th and 5th Australian Divisions moved to the Somme, travelling by rail, in motor lorries or on foot, marching huge distances each day and stopping only to eat cold meals and sleep. Although the Germans seemed unstoppable, the Diggers were excited—surely the German Army would become exhausted and too weak to defend itself.

At the same time, on 26 March, the Allied leaders met at Doullens, just north of Amiens. Field Marshal Haig had earlier requested that the French general, Pétain, send reserves to help the British, but Pétain had refused—he was convinced the Germans were going to launch a new offensive against Paris and he didn't want to deplete his troops. With divisions emerging between the Allies, Field Marshal Ferdinand Foch was put in charge of the Allied front. For the first time since the start of the war, British and French troops were under one commander. Foch's first order was that there were to be no more withdrawals.

The Australians and New Zealanders were frustrated by the retreat—they felt the British had been too quick to flee. While some men accepted that the British had simply been fighting for too long, others felt that the rigid class system robbed soldiers of initiative and that they relied on officers for direction. They disliked the officers even more, believing most were promoted because of money and connections, not ability. The Anzacs' respect had to be earned, and if an officer showed courage they would follow him anywhere. But the typical British officer, they felt, flounced around with gloves, cane and eyepiece, miles behind the front-line and hopelessly out of touch with reality. A popular joke among the men was about an officer overtaking a hare while retreating from the advancing Germans, and yelling, 'Get out of the road you brute and give a man a chance who can run.'

A TERRIBLE THING TO DO

As the Diggers got closer, the land appeared largely deserted, except for refugees carting out their possessions, and the occasional British soldier heading in the opposite direction, telling them that if they kept going they'd 'get killed'.

On 26 March, two brigades of the 4th Australian Division arrived at the village of Hébuterne, 38 kilometres north-west of Amiens, to find it still lightly held by exhausted British troops who'd been fighting and withdrawing for five days. Some wept with relief as the Australians took over.

When the New Zealanders arrived near Beaumont-Hamel close by, the lack of British troops made it obvious they'd come to a gap in the line. Stretching eight kilometres from Beaumont-Hamel to Hébuterne, the gap had to be closed—it was in front of the vital railway junction at Amiens, and this was what the Germans were now aiming for. The New Zealanders marched out to close the gap just as the Germans, flushed with success, were advancing through it. Small fights broke out. In one trench, Private William Morris bayoneted a German soldier. 'It was the only time I used a bayonet, I'm glad it was the last. I was nearly sick. It was a terrible thing to do.'

When the Aucklanders arrived, they were given a Mills bomb each and sent to extend the line towards the Australians at Hébuterne. At dawn, as distant villages burned, fresh German storm troops strolled forward, full of confidence, smoking and laughing, unaware that the gap had been closed. The New Zealanders waited until they were only 45 metres away, then opened fire. The Australian troops in Hébuterne were just as deadly. The Germans tried to advance four more times and, each time, the Diggers shot them down. For Morris, it was a terrible day. The Germans

> sent another lot and he got wiped down the same. Terrible!...They had four deep, cleared the whole thing. Terrible! A terrible thing to happen, isn't it? Just murder.

'YOU WILL HOLD THEM'

With the line secured, the two other brigades of the 4th Division turned their attention to Albert, 15 kilometres from Hébuterne. The town had been captured by the Germans, but instead of pushing on to Amiens and the railway junction, they had stopped to loot and drink.

The brigades marched towards Albert at night, with flares rising and falling along the front-line. Smoking was forbidden;

overhead, the shapes of large Gotha bombers blocked out the stars as they searched for telltale signs of moving troops.

On the morning of 27 March, the Australians looked down a slope, past a railway embankment, at Albert and the small neighbouring village of Dernancourt. The open fields were strewn with the wreckage of three crashed aeroplanes. A riderless horse, covered in blood, galloped back past them, startling hares already bolting from shell explosions. In Albert, the golden Virgin Mary statue still glittered above the smoke from burning houses. The troops moved down to the embankment to relieve a thin, ragged line of Scottish soldiers who'd been fighting and withdrawing for six days. Lieutenant George Mitchell remembered them asking:

'Who are you?'

We told them. 'Forty-eighth Australians.'

'Thank God,' they said. 'You will hold him.'

A German attack the following morning failed. From Albert to Dernancourt, the Australians stood waist-high above the embankment and fired into the advancing troops. One man, Sergeant Stanley McDougall, used a Lewis gun taken from two dead comrades until the barrel grew so hot it burned and blistered his hand. Private Joseph Pitt, a Sydney labourer, worked furiously to construct two functioning guns out of four damaged ones. Others took bombs from prisoners or threw stones. The Germans retreated to the houses of Dernancourt. That night, rain fell as the Australians emptied German packs and found them full of biscuits, letters and packages, some from Australia, stolen from Red

Cross stores. In Dernancourt, the sounds of farm animals in distress could be heard; the famished Germans were killing them for food.

TOO CLOSE TO STOP

Despite the initial British retreat, the withdrawal was over. The Allies now held a continuous line although it was weak in places. Even though the Diggers believed the British had fled too easily, they had slowed the German advance.

The German supply lines were over-extended and the troops exhausted, but General Ludendorff had come too close to Amiens to stop. Over the next five days, the Germans attempted to split General Gough's weakened British 5th Army from the French at Villers-Bretonneux, another town close to Amiens. During this time, an Australian battalion helped hold the line after British troops left their positions, while the New Zealanders launched a successful attack near Hébuterne that saw the Germans driven back for the first time since 21 March.

But on 4 April the 35th Battalion of the Australian 9th Brigade was forced into retreat through Villers-Bretonneux after British troops on either side panicked and fell back. The last Australians in the area, the 36th Battalion, were told to advance until stopped, then to 'hold on at all costs'. Before marching out, Lieutenant Colonel John Milne, the battalion commander, looked at his men and said, 'Goodbye, boys, it's neck or nothing.' When the five waves of advancing German troops spotted the fast-moving Australians, they took cover in nearby woods and opened fire. The Australians also took cover, and a soldier in the uniform of a British officer arrived at one post and ordered the men to withdraw. The lance corporal in charge of the post asked for papers, but when the officer had none and couldn't prove his identity, the lance corporal shot him, believing he was a German. Whether he was or not was never established.

Soldiers of the 36th Battalion fell thickly, but the survivors rushed on in small groups, one party giving covering fire as another raced forward. Soon the Germans began to break, and when the British cavalry rode forward with swords and lances drawn, some of the retiring 35th Battalion joined them to form a solid line in front of Villers-Bretonneux. The town, for now, was held.

The next day, three German divisions attacked the Australians holding the railway embankment near Albert. They surged through a gap in the line at the railway bridge—heavy shelling had killed all the men—and moved up the slope, hauling up their artillery to fire directly into any post that resisted. The Australian artillery reply was weak—only two guns had ammunition left—so the Diggers left their wounded and retreated to a trench at the top of the slope. The wounded were taken prisoner. Some were well cared for, others weren't. When one German officer asked a group who they were, Private Frank Curtis replied, 'Australians.' The officer shot him in the stomach.

But the Germans failed to break through. They had captured the railway embankment but had run out of troops and energy. As German soldiers paid their respects by erecting rough wooden crosses for two Australian dead with the epitaph 'Here lies a brave English warrior,' Ludendorff paused the Somme offensive and turned his attention to Flanders.

BACKS TO THE WALL

Ludendorff's second attack—Operation Georgette—was launched in Flanders, where many Allied troops had just arrived to recover from the Somme. This attack was as brutal, and the consequences as devastating. Armentières, Messines, Bullecourt and Passchendaele—every metre of territory the British, New Zealanders and Australians had fought and died for in 1917, and more, fell. Soon Hazebrouck, a major railway centre that supplied half the Flanders area with food and ammunition, was within a day's march of the Germans. As the 1st Australian Division moved to Hazebrouck, Field Marshal Haig appealed to his troops:

> Every position must be held to the last man...With our backs to the wall, and believing in the justice of our cause, each one of us must fight on to the end.

Arriving at Hazebrouck station on 12 April, the Australians marched forward with a pannikin of hot cocoa and dug a second line of trenches six miles in front of Hazebrouck. The following day, the Germans continued to advance and, with British troops retreating past them, the Australians found that their trenches had become the front-line.

On the morning of 14 April, the advancing German waves made easy targets. One soldier said it was 'like firing at a whole haystack—one could not miss.' But on 16 April, two New Zealand companies of the 2nd Entrenching Battalion had a different experience in a village next to the Australians. The men—mostly new to France and expecting to dig trenches, not fight—found themselves surrounded by Germans. After the British retreated, one company fought its way back, but in the other over 100 men surrendered—the largest number of New Zealanders to be taken prisoner at one time.

Despite the rapid German advances, the British eventually re-established their line. Hazebrouck was safe. With Operation Georgette slowly grinding to a halt, Ludendorff once again turned his attention back to the Somme.

VILLERS-BRETONNEUX

At the Somme, British and Australian troops dug new defensive positions and lived off pigs, ducks, fish and champagne taken from abandoned villages. If they spotted a flying pigeon, they shot it down. It was a brief respite; the Australians, who now held 27 kilometres of the front, from Hangard to Albert, expected an attack—reports and surveillance indicated a German build-up. On the night of 17 April, the Germans fired over 20,000 shells into Villers-Bretonneux, drenching the area in gas which soaked the troops' clothes. When the Allies removed their masks, the gas got into their eyes and lungs. Hundreds stumbled out of Villers-Bretonneux, their eyes streaming and closing over. No advance followed but signs kept pointing to an attack.

Overhead, Captain Richthofen and his Flying Circus

fought the British for air supremacy. On 21 April the Red Baron flew low over the Allied lines, chasing a scout biplane. The Australians fired up at him as he passed over them. Suddenly the Red Baron's machine swerved, dived and crashed. Germany's greatest war ace was dead, shot through the heart, most likely by one of the Australians who rushed over to strip him and his triplane for souvenirs.

That afternoon, as German deserters talked of a coming offensive, British troops replaced the Australians in front of Villers-Bretonneux. They were mostly under 19 years old, young men who wouldn't have been accepted into the army in 1914. One Australian wrote in his diary that

> for two days companies of infantry have been passing us on the roads—companies of children, English children; pink faced, round cheeked children, flushed under the weight of their unaccustomed packs, with their steel helmets on the back of their heads and the strap hanging loosely on their rounded baby chins.

The British War Council, disillusioned with Haig after Passchendaele, had been withholding reinforcements for fear he would use them to capture yet another shell-holed village. But with British divisions weak after the German attacks, the council sent the reinforcements. Rather than giving them experience in quiet areas, the British commanders rushed them to critical zones. When, on 24 April, 13 three-metre-high German tanks loomed out of a dense mist after a heavy bombardment of gas and high explosives, most of the boy-soldiers fled, and, although the Germans had to fight from house to house, Villers-Bretonneux was captured.

Two brigades of the 4th and 5th Divisions were ordered up to retake the village. The British commanders wanted an immediate attack, but the commander of the 13th Brigade, Brigadier General Thomas Glasgow, refused, saying the men would be slaughtered in the daylight. The British insisted until Glasgow replied, 'If it was God-Almighty who gave the order we couldn't do it in daylight.'

While the men wrote letters, 'posted' them in a sandbag for delivery and drank hot tea, their commanders finalised the plan. The two brigades—the 15th under Brigadier General Elliot and the 13th under Glasgow—were to skirt the village and then meet in front of it to prevent German reinforcements from entering and those inside from leaving.

NEW WAVES ALWAYS COME ON CHEERING

It was dark when the 13th Brigade waited at the jumping-off point. Captain Billy Harburn, commander of one of the companies in the 51st Battalion, told his men to ignore the German-held wood and village houses on their left, and that nothing was to stop them getting to their objective. 'Kill every bloody German you see, we don't want any prisoners and God bless you.' The sky glowed red under the thudding British bombardment as soldiers of the 51st and 52nd Battalions moved slowly forward, freezing each time flares lit the night. Then German machine guns churned to life.

The 51st Battalion was in trouble; the Germans in the woods fired flare after flare, silhouetting them against the skyline. The troops staggered on through gunfire, then halted. Groups of men half-knelt on the slope, as if they were praying, but they were all dead. Lieutenant Clifford Sadlier and Sergeant Charles Stokes, both from Subiaco, Western Australia, knew they couldn't move until the Germans in the woods were silenced. They gathered as many bombs as they could and then, leading the survivors, charged into the trees towards the bursts of phosphorescent tracer bullets flickering in straight, steady streams through the trees. Stumbling in the dark, they bombed their way from gun to gun, until the woods grew silent.

But as the Australians continued their advance, German machine-gunners in a trench in front of them opened fire. The men stalled, but surged forward again at the whistle-blow of an officer, picking their way over the barbed wire and rushing the trench. The Australians advanced another 900 metres, until eight further gunners set up in shell holes opened fire.

The Germans fired until they were down to their last belt of ammunition. Many of the Australians, rushing forward in groups under cover of their Lewis gunners, were killed, but, as witnessed by a German officer, Sergeant Major Elfeldt, 'New waves always come on cheering in their place and rush forward into our machine-gun fire.' As the ammunition ran out, the Australians let out a final wild yell and chased the Germans until forced to a halt. They were 250 metres short of their final objective, and, although they weren't able to join with the 15th Brigade in front of Villers-Bretonneux, the brigade machine-gunners instead trained their guns across the gap.

THERE THEY GO

Like the 13th Brigade on the right, the three battalions of the 15th Brigade had also lined up as houses burned in Villers-Bretonneux. It was just past midnight on 25 April, and some men smiled at each other and muttered, 'It's Anzac Day'—taking this as a good omen. But they too were spotted. The Germans opened fire. The Australians broke into a roar and surged forward, screaming into the flare-lit dark. They charged machine guns frontally, killing the crew. Any German who tried to surrender was killed and those found hiding were bayoneted. There were calls of 'There they go, there they go!'—the 15th Brigade chased any who fled; their hands and rifles became slippery with blood.

By 4 a.m., machine guns of both brigades covered the gap in front of Villers-Bretonneux, and after several British and Australian companies cleared the village, the troops scavenged for souvenirs. Men played billiards in a mansion while bullets pinged through the window. Others changed their lice-ridden underwear for fancy lingerie, much to the surprise of the nurses when some were later wounded.

The German advance had failed. The battle, on the anniversary of the landing at Gallipoli in 1915, had left 1500 Australians dead or wounded. The sandbag of letters the men had written prior to the attack was found beside the body of a dead soldier, the envelopes stained with blood. It was Lieutenant Mitchell's duty to read the letters:

> War hardened as I was, the task shook me—these last lines of the fallen. Cheering words to mothers in far-off sunny places, loving thoughts to wives, to children, to sweethearts. A little longing of the writers crept through. Sometimes there was a hint of the knowledge of the approach of the reaper. My eyes were wet, long before I had finished.

On 3 May, in the moonlight, Mitchell 'hopped the bags' again. He was in a bad mood; he was to attack a German-held wood opposite Villers-Bretonneux with 'untrained rabble' against seasoned troops. Without conscription, the Australian reinforcement numbers were running low, so men who'd enlisted into non-combat roles were being used to fill up the thinning ranks. While veteran troops had drunk wine with French soldiers, Mitchell had trained the reinforcements to load a rifle. Now, in the flare light, the inexperienced troops grouped together as a German 'with a voice like a bull' barked at his machine-gunners to fire. The attack quickly failed.

When stretcher-bearers raced out waving white clothes in place of Red Cross flags, a tall German officer confronted them, asking them if they wanted to surrender.

The Australians said, 'Surrender be—.'

'I do not understand French. Talk in English,' he replied.

Mitchell met the German officer in the middle of

no-man's-land, and, after saluting each other, they agreed to a 20-minute truce. After two hours, the two men met again. Mitchell declined an offer of more time, and they returned to their lines. Once there, they met each other's gaze before dropping into their trenches.

The Spring Offensive was over. Although the Germans had gained land—most of it the same land they'd occupied in 1914—this was no longer enough to win the war. They'd failed to defeat the British and their crack troops had been shot down leading the advances. They still had more divisions on the Western Front than the Allies, but they hadn't defeated the British before the Americans arrived.

KILLED IN ACTION

PRIVATE FRANK CURTIS
Farmer. 5 April 1918

LIEUTENANT COLONEL JOHN MILNE
Engineer. 12 April 1918

PRIVATE CHARLES BIRD
Pipe moulder. 1 September 1918

CHAPTER ELEVEN

BLACK DAYS, 1918

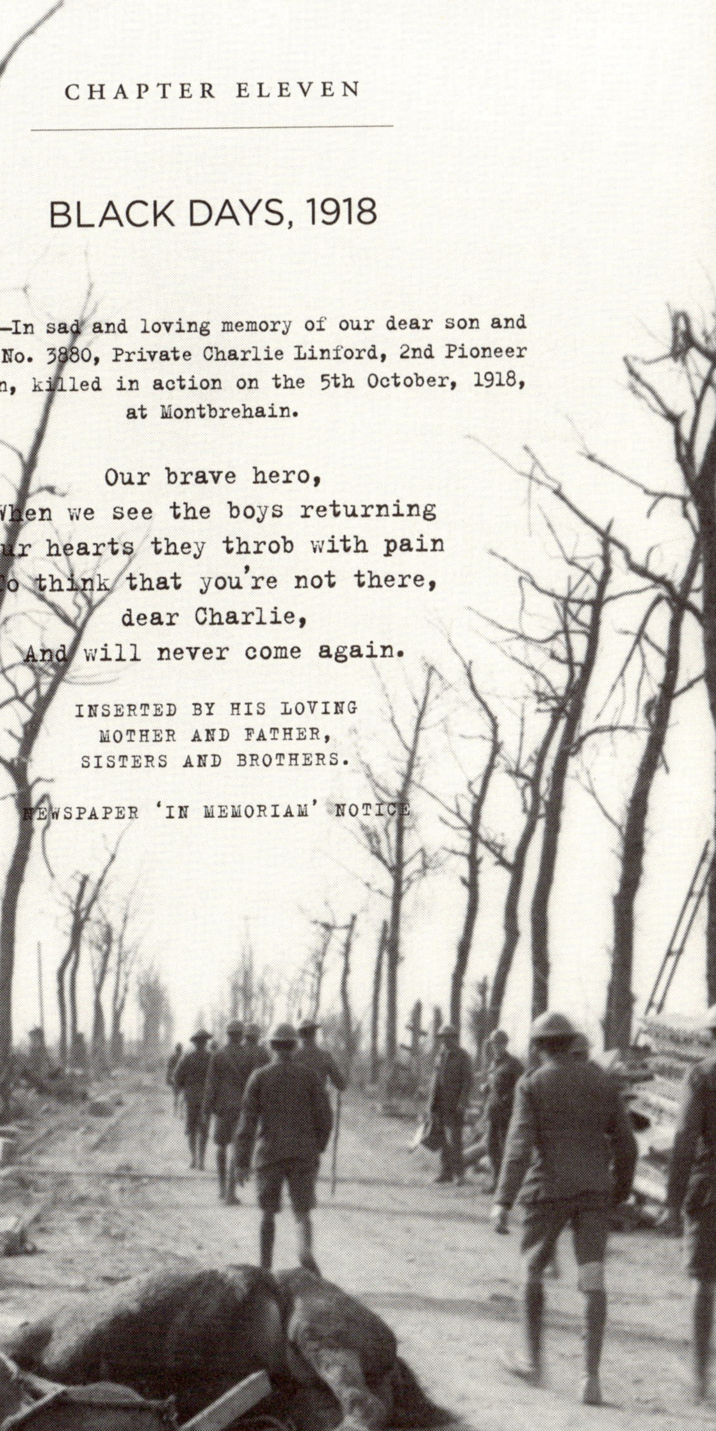

LINFORD—In sad and loving memory of our dear son and brother, No. 3880, Private Charlie Linford, 2nd Pioneer Battalion, killed in action on the 5th October, 1918, at Montbrehain.

Our brave hero,
When we see the boys returning
Our hearts they throb with pain
To think that you're not there,
dear Charlie,
And will never come again.

INSERTED BY HIS LOVING
MOTHER AND FATHER,
SISTERS AND BROTHERS.

NEWSPAPER 'IN MEMORIAM' NOTICE

WHILE THE BRITISH divisions recovered from the Spring Offensive, the Australians and New Zealanders welcomed the quiet arrival of better weather at the Somme and Flanders. They bathed in streams, bombed for fish, played two-up, wrote letters home, and shot hares and goats to eat. Veterans who'd served at Gallipoli now wore a golden 'A' sewn to their tunic.

Not content with resting, the Diggers made sure that their sectors at Hazebrouck, Amiens and Hébuterne became the liveliest on the front. Using the hedges in Flanders and the high wild crops growing in the Somme no-man's-land as cover, they began what became known as 'peaceful penetration'. On hot dry days, they stole across no-man's-land into the enemy trenches, killing or kidnapping sentries. To the troops who came up to relieve the posts, these men seemed to have just disappeared. A history of one German sector recorded that

> we have the Australians opposite us (200 metres away) and they are very quick and cunning. They glide about in the night like cats, and come right up to our trenches without our seeing them. Last night they were in our trenches and killed two men and dragged one away with them.

Another history said: 'They lay opposite us, exceptionally good Australian troops, who kept us on tenterhooks with their all night activity.' Commanders began to complain about being put opposite the Australians, and referred to their time as 'bloody'. According to a German intelligence report the New Zealanders were a 'good assault division' with a

> very strongly developed individual self-confidence... and a specially pronounced hatred of the Germans. The Division prides itself on taking few prisoners.

Propaganda claimed the New Zealanders were cannibals.

While the Allies waited for the next blow, the Australians launched small attacks, capturing the village of Ville-sur-Ancre on 19 May. Eight days later, the Germans forced the French back 50 kilometres, to within 56 kilometres of Paris, before running out of steam. Then, on 10 June, the Australians stormed Morlancourt at the Somme, capturing 325 Germans and leaving their divisional commander worried that if 'a complete battalion had been wiped out' in a few minutes, worse could happen.

A MORALE BOOST

It had now been over a year since the United States had declared war, but, as they didn't have enough equipment or training, their force had been slow to arrive. The first troops had landed in June 1917, but for training only—the American General John Pershing didn't want them to fight until fully trained or to be split up among the French and British Armies. He wanted a single American force.

The slowness of the Americans' arrival and training frustrated the other Allies. But by June 1918, there were eight American divisions in France, and tens of thousands more troops were arriving each month—74,000 had landed in May and June alone.

The Australians had expected the Americans to boast that

they'd win the war, but none did; they were serious, and keen to learn from those who'd been through it already. While the Americans' arrival boosted morale, they were frequently and humorously reminded of how late they'd turned up. One story from late 1917 had a group of Americans, Australians and New Zealanders eating in a cafe in Paris. The Americans noticed the similarity between their hats and those of the New Zealand troops. When the New Zealanders left, they asked who they were, saying, 'They're not Americans.'

The Australians replied, 'No, you silly Blighters, they're soldiers.'

CHANGES

After the collapse of the 5th Army during the Spring Offensive, Field Marshal Haig replaced General Gough with General Birdwood, and Monash—now promoted to lieutenant general—became the new commander of the Australian divisions. On taking over, Monash began preparing for the first major Allied offensive since the Third Battle of Ypres. He was a studious planner who believed the soldiers' role was to secure objectives, not smash through the line—that was the job of artillery, aeroplanes and tanks. Many of his divisional commanders still opposed tanks after Bullecourt, but the new Mark Vs were now faster than a running soldier, could turn without stopping first and could also reverse. The Australian soldiers attended tank demonstrations, and climbed onto them for joyrides, drove them and chalked pet names on their iron sides.

New Zealand soldiers beneath a sign saying 'The Cannibals Paradise Supply Den Beware'. Alexander Turnbull Library G-13460-1/2

On 4 July, the Australians advanced to capture Le Hamel, which would straighten their line. Monash had planned it down to the last minute. Tanks and several American companies would assist the depleted 2nd, 3rd and 4th Divisions—some companies were down to 80 men after the Spring Offensive, an outbreak of a mild version of the Spanish flu and lack of reinforcements. For days, the enemy front-line had been bombed with smoke and gas shells so that whenever the smoke shells burst, the Germans would suspect gas and put on their masks, which made it difficult to breathe or see, let alone fight.

At zero hour, as aeroplanes bombed Le Hamel, over 5500 troops strolled forward through the high crops alongside 60 tanks. Overhead, ammunition was parachuted to chosen points, or where machine-gun crews had laid V-shaped white cloth in cleared wheat. The artillery fired smoke and high explosives, but this time, no gas.

Around Le Hamel, the Germans were disorientated. Many still wore their gasmasks, believing, as Monash had hoped, that there was gas mingled with the smoke. Their machine-gunners, firing too high, refused to surrender until outflanked or crushed by tanks. Stretcher-bearers and orderlies manning one company headquarters fought from a dugout until phosphorus bombs set it on fire, killing everyone inside. Others quickly surrendered. The German infantry, the Australians were beginning to note, were quicker to surrender or flee than their machine-gunners, who would often fire until killed. Hundreds of soldiers were captured in the cellars of Le Hamel, still wearing gasmasks and unaware that a battle had been raging outside.

Ninety-three minutes after zero hour, the battle was over. Monash's tactics had worked. Over 1600 Germans had surrendered, and their troops were demoralised. The Spring Offensive and the Spanish flu had also decimated their companies—some were down to 50 men—and many of the reinforcements were teenagers, older men from the Eastern Front, or strikers and prisoners, some of whom took off in the first few days. They had built few dugouts and, for the first time, were using their own trenches for toilets. Harvest failures and the blockade of German ports, which prevented food supplies getting in, meant the troops were surviving on turnips and flesh stripped from dead horses. Despite over 1000 Australians and 176 Americans having been killed or wounded, the Australians were convinced they could have gone further and captured the German artillery.

On 15 July, another German attempt to threaten Paris failed after Pershing allowed two American divisions to fight alongside the French. After being pushed back nine kilometres, with 20,000 taken prisoner, the German leaders realised that the attempt to reach a favourable peace settlement through military victory had failed. The best they could hope for now was a stalemate at the negotiating table, but the British and French had little interest in a compromised peace. Knowing the Germans wouldn't willingly choose to surrender unconditionally, the Allies planned their next major offensive.

THE HUNDRED DAYS OFFENSIVE

The first of many joint operations of the Hundred Days Offensive began at the Somme on 8 August, followed by a three-day attack on 21 August. Secrecy was now considered essential for victory. The sky was filled with hundreds of British aeroplanes fighting to keep German observation aeroplanes away. Canadian troops were secretly moved down from Arras. Soldiers' pay books were stamped with the words 'keep your mouths shut', and no movement was allowed during the day.

In battles for Amiens and Albert, the Diggers advanced behind barrages of 'daisy cutter' shells that exploded on impact. According to Australian Lieutenant Harold Binder, it was like 'being behind a curtain of rushing noise'. New Zealander Second Lieutenant Robert Gilkison found the creeping barrage 'a wonderful sound' and he 'almost pitied the Germans on the receiving end'.

In the mist and smoke, soldiers slipped through the German lines. One second lieutenant, William Sievers, called in artillery fire to shatter a threatening counterattack. Many Germans fled or surrendered, while machine-gunners were either outflanked or crushed by tanks. Those retreating told the reserves marching forward that 'everything is lost.'

For the Germans, 8 August was a black day—over 13,000 prisoners were captured, close to 8000 by the Australians. The war resources of the Allies now far outnumbered those of the Germans—on that day, 1900 aeroplanes had flown against 365, and 540 tanks had advanced against none.

The battles continued relentlessly. After shooting and bombing through Loupart Wood and Grevillers village, the New Zealanders failed to capture Bapaume, but, on 29 August, after German flares and machine-gun fire became less frequent, New Zealand patrols entered Bapaume to find it abandoned. The Germans were gone; the Canadians had broken their line at Arras, forcing them into a retreat to the Hindenburg Line.

The New Zealanders pursued them, calling in artillery fire and tanks to destroy machine-gun nests that had been set up to slow pursuers. The Germans left booby traps behind: leaking gas shells were hidden in dugouts; bombs were planted under corpses or in doorways. One trap was placed under a pile of firewood in an abandoned trench. When a young New Zealand soldier lit it for warmth, the explosion blew both his legs off. Rifleman Arthur Ross was

> sure he did not know his legs were gone. Someone gave him a cigarette and lit it for him…Poor devil, he just bled to death, in three minutes he was dead.

The Australian pursuit of the Germans ended at the dense barbed-wire entanglements of Mont St. Quentin and the moated and walled town of Péronne, 18 kilometres in front of the Hindenburg Line. Although the Australians were exhausted, Monash wanted the area captured before the Germans became too firmly entrenched.

At 5 a.m. on 31 August, the depleted companies charged Mont St. Quentin, yelling like a 'lot of bushrangers' to make up for their lack of men. The Germans said that 'it all happened like lightning', and surrendered in large numbers. Despite this, a determined counterattack saw the Mont recaptured.

That afternoon, down at the Somme River, fresh Australian troops passed cinematographers filming them. Ambulance wagons drove back with the wounded, and men stepped over the dead, while others huddled below banks, singing and yelling 'overs' at the German gunners whenever their shells passed over and burst harmlessly in the river.

In drizzling rain on 1 September, the Australians quickly recaptured Mont St. Quentin, but the moated fortress of Péronne took longer. Elite German Guard troops were both inside and outside the walls, and the town was surrounded by bands of wire. Australian Lewis gunners forced those outside to take cover as men cut the wire or tore out the pickets with their hands. Some Germans kept firing—one gun had been firing so rapidly that the water to keep it cool was boiling—but the Australians got through, then chased the fleeing Germans so quickly that the troops inside Péronne couldn't open fire for fear of hitting their own men. With most of the defenders caught sheltering in cellars, the town was soon in Australian hands—one platoon drank hot coffee in a cellar with their prisoners.

TO THE HINDENBURG LINE

The Australians, New Zealanders and British continued to pursue the Germans as they withdrew to the Hindenburg

Line. The horizon was streaked with pillars of smoke from burning villages; bridges were destroyed and crossroads mined. The men passed forgotten Roman forts, stormed villages and outflanked German machine-gun posts, some set up in disabled German tanks to slow the chase.

The advance moved at a speed unthinkable six months earlier. From gains of 1300 metres, the Allies now advanced in kilometres. By the end of August, they had advanced 40 kilometres on a 113-kilometre front, retaking the lost Somme ground. But as the Australians reached the first of the four trenches of the Hindenburg Line on 10 September, the New Zealanders passing Havrincourt Woods were halted at Trescault Ridge—a strategic height five kilometres in front of the Hindenburg Line—by an elite Jaeger Division with orders to hold the ground at all costs. Over two days, bomb battles raged up trenches as German gas and shells 'burnt the grass and earth black'. Then, on 12 September, during the first phase of the Battle of Havrincourt-Epehy, the Diggers won parts of Trescault Ridge before losing it again when the Jaegers counterattacked with flamethrowers.

Six days later, the Australians, 20 kilometres south of the New Zealanders, took part in the final phase of the Havrincourt-Epehy battle. The Germans occupied four trenches. The first two were old British trenches, the next was the Hindenburg Outpost Line, then behind a deep canal was the Hindenburg Line itself. The Allies knew that even if they captured the first three, the canal would be a major obstacle. However, for five kilometres it ran underground through the Bellicourt Tunnel, and even though the Germans had heavily wired the land above it, this was the logical place to try to break through. Across a 27-kilometre front, the British planned to advance to the Outpost Line. In the middle, four brigades from the 1st and 4th Australian Divisions would form the spearhead, despite their already depleted numbers being further reduced—two months' leave back home had been granted to soldiers who'd enlisted in 1914.

On 18 September, the Australians, forbidden to smoke or make any noise, grew tense as 'one minute' was whispered down the line. In a thick mist, the first and second trenches and the Hindenburg Outpost Line were quickly overrun, despite being strongly held. The Germans weren't putting up a fight; large numbers surrendered, some even running towards the Australians, asking 'Which way?', though Sergeant Joseph Holt, a well-known Queensland footballer, was rounding up a bunch of prisoners when one of them pulled out a revolver and killed him. Impressed with the Australians' speed and skill, a captured German officer remarked, 'All I can say is you are some bloody soldiers!' But veteran Australian soldiers knew that if the Germans had put up a fight, they wouldn't have stood a chance.

The Australians had captured most of the Outpost Line in front of them, but the British hadn't seized the vital section in front of the Bellicourt Tunnel. When the exhausted Australians of two battalions—who were expecting to be relieved from the front-line—were ordered to assist the British in capturing this section, some of the men refused, saying they were being 'put in to do other people's work' and weren't 'getting a fair deal'. In all, 119 men walked away from the front, and despite another commander offering to help, the attack still failed. The troops who'd refused to fight were found guilty of desertion, but not mutiny—an offence more likely to be punishable by death.

TO THE LAST LINE

With German morale obviously low—110,000 soldiers had deserted in August alone—Field Marshal Foch, the Allies' supreme commander, ordered the troops to strike at different times and different locations along the Hindenburg Line after brief but brutal artillery barrages. The Germans were driven back six kilometres at Reims. Trescault Ridge was captured. In Flanders, a combined force of Belgian, French and British troops drove the Germans back past Passchendaele Ridge, gaining in one attack what had taken months in 1917. But the Americans failed to capture the Outpost Line in front of Bellicourt Tunnel. On the morning of 29 September, the Allies attacked again at Bellicourt.

The main planning had fallen to Major General Monash, and he had decided to use two American divisions to capture the Outpost Line, cross over it and seize the Hindenburg Line. The 3rd and 5th Australian Divisions would then pass on and capture the last German defence line—the Beaurevoir Line—three kilometres on. General Rawlinson, commander of the 4th Army which included the Australian Corps, was concerned about the narrow front. He included the 46th

British Division in the attack—they were to use flotation devices to cross the canal before attacking.

At zero hour, according to Sergeant Walter Downing, the ground quivered with the 'recoil of thousands of guns. The din was ear-splitting. One could not hear one's own voice.' The battlefield was covered in smoke. Three hours later, the 3rd and 5th Divisions marched out through heavily gassed areas to secure the last line, the sun glinting off the glass in their goggles. They passed dead and wounded Americans in the trampled wheat. Ahead of them, British tanks burned. The Americans on the left had again failed to overcome the Outpost Line, forcing the Australians to fight for an area they were meant to be just passing through. American bodies lay everywhere and, as German gunners swept the land in front of the Outpost Line, the left flank of the Australian advance was halted.

On the right, the Americans had overrun the Hindenburg Line and here the Australians kept going, passing bodies lying thick in front of machine-gun posts. They kept their distance from the tanks, which drew intense artillery fire, and fought on until they looked out over a seemingly empty land. Joined by soldiers of the 46th British Division, who'd swum across the canal, they pushed on together until, exhausted and isolated, they dug in short of the Beaurevoir Line.

BREAKING THE BEAUREVOIR

Nearby, under a fingernail moon, the New Zealanders had followed up the British success at Trescault Ridge and cleared the ruins of the village of La Vacquerie. They'd bombed up the intricate web of the Hindenburg trenches, until, in the cool breeze of dawn, they looked down over a canal to the unscathed Beaurevoir Line behind it. Beyond that, smoke from burning dumps billowed above the lofty towers and spires of Cambrai. New Zealand machine-gunners fired down at horses and Germans trying to haul away their artillery.

With the Hindenburg Line broken, the Germans were in retreat. General Ludendorff told the Kaiser that the war was lost and to seek an armistice with the Allies before his army was destroyed.

On 3 October, British and Australian troops broke through the Beaurevoir Line. Sergeant James Seivewright, a labourer from Queensland, crawled under a band of uncut wire and single-handedly captured a post of 52 men. The Germans were in poor spirits; if they'd resisted, the Australians would have been shot down in front of the wire by the 50 machine guns facing the approach.

With this section of the Beaurevoir Line secure, Field Marshal Haig ordered that villages beyond it be captured so he could finally send his cavalry through. On 5 October, the 6th Brigade of the 2nd Australian Division set out to capture Montbrehain. The 21st and 24th Battalions and 2nd Pioneer Battalion, who were not trained to fight as infantry, followed the churning dust and smoke of the creeping barrage, but the Germans stayed at their guns. Under cover from their Lewis gunners, the men charged in rushes until the Germans were killed or captured. One prisoner told his captors that they were 'sick of the war and had they known Australians were attacking they would not have fought at all'.

At other strong points in the village, the Germans kept fighting. When a machine-gun post pinned a group of Australians down, Sergeant Major George Cumming tried to lead a charge to overcome it, but was killed. Others who showed themselves were also picked off. But when a sergeant got to within 18 metres of the strong point and opened fire with his Lewis gun, Lieutenant George Ingram rushed the post, killing or capturing 40 Germans. With more machine guns preventing Ingram from moving on, he and his men caught the attention of a nearby tank. After following it, Ingram shot several more soldiers and captured over 60 prisoners and 40 guns. For his actions, he was later awarded the Victoria Cross, the last of 54 Australians to be awarded the decoration on the Western Front. As the Australians continued to capture the village, house by house, local villagers came out of their cellars to greet them.

The capture of Montbrehain was a brilliant success, though in the short, brutal fight 430 men had been killed or wounded. As the divisions were withdrawn for a much-needed rest, none of the Australians realised this would be their last battle on the Western Front.

CRUMBLING

The day before, the German chancellor had sent a diplomatic note to the United States' president seeking an armistice, but meanwhile Ludendorff's opinion of the state of his army had changed—the British in Flanders and the French and Americans in the Verdun sector had been stopped and with only the British 4th Army making any progress, he became convinced that the German Army could fight on new defensive lines to get a better peace deal. So, as the bulk of his forces withdrew back to new lines, skeleton forces—like those facing the New Zealanders behind 45 metres of wire at the Beaurevoir Line—prepared to stall the British pursuit.

Field Marshal Foch, wanting to prevent the Germans prolonging the war, ordered a succession of attacks along the Western Front. At dawn on 8 October, the 4th Army, and the New Zealanders with the 3rd Army, attacked and broke the Beaurevoir Line in their sector, then chased the crumbling German Army for three days, giving them no time to establish a new line of defence.

When not fighting, the New Zealanders ate boiled swedes from the villagers' gardens to supplement their rations. In the frosty mornings, they stamped their feet to warm themselves, then followed creeping barrages across largely abandoned land. In some places, the Germans stood their ground and fought. Private J. Ward's rifle was shot away, so he picked up a shovel and rejoined the advance, killing three with it. The New Zealanders took pot shots at the fleeing troops, and in front of Fontaine village they watched a single German machine-gunner in the church spire shoot down a British cavalry charge.

On 17 October, as the British in Flanders forced the

Germans back from the Belgian coast and the French and Americans attacked again in the Verdun sector, the New Zealanders and British fought across the heavily defended River Selle. The New Zealanders pursued the Germans until, on 31 October, the ramparts of the ancient and famous Le Quesnoy fortress lay in front of them, hidden by trees. In two weeks, the New Zealanders, with British divisions on either side of them, had advanced 18 kilometres.

THE FORTRESS OF LE QUESNOY

Over the next four days, the New Zealanders moved closer to the town, taking prisoners and burying the dead. The British carted in wagonloads of corpses, each one sewn in a blanket, then laid them in two rows, side by side, in a mass grave. They covered them with a layer of earth, then laid another row on top. The German dead were dragged by their heels and thrown into the nearest trench, then covered with dirt.

Everything was collapsing around the Germans. Bulgaria and Turkey had conceded defeat on 20 October. When Austria–Hungary sought peace on 28 October, German civilians called for peace at any price, and sailors mutinied when ordered to set out to fight the British again.

At dawn on 4 November, in the final Allied offensive, the New Zealanders set out to capture the 11th-century fortress town of Le Quesnoy. The Germans had machine guns on top of the nine-metre-high inner rampart, as well as among the trees on man-made 'islands' that divided the outer moat. The town was filled with civilians and historic buildings, so it was decided that the artillery would carefully explode oil drums and smoke shells on the ramparts to give the infantry cover. The New Zealanders moved up on either side of the town, overrunning machine-gunners. While several battalions tried to break through the fortress, others advanced kilometres past it, effectively cutting off the Germans inside. As they advanced, villagers gave them gifts of coffee and fruit and large numbers of Germans surrendered.

The attempt to capture the fortress itself had been frustrated. German machine-gunners had pinned down the New Zealanders. Second Lieutenant Francis Evans and four others managed to scale an 'island' rampart, then raced through the trees towards the dry inner moat and inner rampart wall, until they were spotted. Taking cover in a shallow hole, they waited for the gunfire to cease. When it did, Evans scrambled out, but the machine-gunner was waiting, and after a short burst of bullets Evans rolled back into the hole, shot in the head. Another of the soldiers tried to fire his Lewis gun, but was also killed, leaving the remaining three to wait in the hole with their dead comrades for the next six hours.

With the town surrounded, the New Zealand commander sent German prisoners across to explain the hopelessness of the situation. Only one group returned, saying the troops were willing to surrender but the officers wouldn't let them. In the early afternoon, an aeroplane dropped a message requesting the Germans surrender, but their machine-gunners kept firing. While the New Zealand Lewis gunners and mortar teams forced the Germans to take cover, Second

Lieutenants Leslie Averill and Harold Kerr got to the inner rampart, leaned a scaling ladder against it and scrambled up. At the top, Averill fired at two Germans running away in panic, then he and Kerr strode down the grass slope into the town, shooting at a crowd of soldiers who rushed for cover. Over 700 Germans surrendered peacefully. When the New Zealanders marched through the open gates, the locals embraced them and gave them flowers and cakes. Fifty New Zealanders had been killed and another 238 had been wounded.

The following night, the second of the offensive, another 20 New Zealanders were killed as they fought from tree to tree through a dense forest with heavy rain falling. It was the New Zealanders' last battle. The Germans were now broken and in forced retreat, leaving behind vast quantities of material and abandoned trains. British aeroplanes flew over an empty land; there was no one left to shoot at.

In Germany, revolution had broken out. Workers took to the streets and demanded that the Kaiser step down, and when German soldiers refused to shoot the workers, the Kaiser was replaced. The new leader immediately accepted the harsh armistice terms—the terms that General Ludendorff had earlier hoped would inspire the German people to fight on.

A QUIET END

The armistice to end the Great War was signed in a railway carriage on 11 November, coming into effect at 11 a.m. The 1st and 4th Australian Divisions returned to the Western

Front after their long rest to find it eerily quiet; not one gun was firing. The war to end all wars was over. Nearly 10 million people had been killed.

It was a foggy, sunless day. On hearing the news, the soldiers at the front didn't cheer. For Gunner Bert Stokes, 'it was just a relief, we didn't celebrate at all.' According to New Zealander Private James Weir, 'everyone was so dog tired. We had gone beyond hope. It wouldn't sink in. We couldn't care less.' 'Fancy no more shells,' wrote Private James McKenzie, 'no more bullets, no more sleeping in dirty wet trenches etc. I was on the verge of tears thinking of putting in another winter on the line...' For Lieutenant George Mitchell 'it all seemed unreal...Our known world had slipped from us.' In military camps and towns away from the front the mood was more celebratory. Sergeant Eric Evans wrote in his diary:

> The fighting is finished. Hurrah! My letters which I wrote to be posted after my death will now be of no use. Thank God. The war has finished and we have won. Hurrah!

KILLED IN ACTION

SERGEANT JOSEPH HOLT
Railway employee. 18 September 1918

SERGEANT MAJOR GEORGE CUMMING
Cellarman. 5 October 1918

PRIVATE CHARLIE LINFORD
Blacksmith. 5 October 1918

SECOND LIEUTENANT FRANCIS EVANS
Clerk. 4 November 1918

CHAPTER TWELVE

THE WAR TO END ALL WARS

FERN SEED (extract)

From Hébuterne to Havrincourt
The map is wet with tears —
And women proudly, blindly turn
To face the barren years.

BY D. H. L., 8 NOVEMBER 1918

WHEN THE NEWS reached New Zealand and Australia, church, factory and ship bells tolled and people poured into the streets to celebrate. The troops were eager to return home but they had a long wait. On 28 November, the New Zealanders marched through French and Belgian villages, which were draped in welcome banners and strewn with flowers, en route to Germany and occupation. As they crossed the River Rhine, the German crowds were silent and grim. It didn't take long for the men to befriend the locals, and the more they came to know them, the more they realised the waste of war. Diggers sat with German veterans in cafes and spoke of the mud of Passchendaele.

Slowly, the soldiers were shipped back to New Zealand. Those who'd served the longest and married men were sent first. By 25 March 1919, the last of the New Zealand troops were demobilised.

The Australians, shipped to England, underwent civilian training as they waited to be sent back on a 'first to come, first to go' basis. With transports hard to find, the slowness frustrated them—they caused so much disturbance in London that the British prime minister wanted them sent home as quickly as possible, but, even so, the last Australian troops didn't return until September 1919.

HOMEWARD BOUND

The Australians and New Zealanders trickled back to countries that were battling the ravages of Spanish flu—a deadly virus that in three days killed soldiers who'd survived the whole war. Several ships arriving home were not allowed to dock immediately for fear of spreading the illness; the men were kept in quarantine, much to their anger. Some homecomings were major affairs, others less so; people were preoccupied with the flu.

For many, returning home was harder than expected. Gunner Bert Stokes felt he 'was just a soldier who'd come back from war'. Everything he'd done, everything he'd known and been part of were finished, and he would have to start again. The governments tried to help: injured soldiers were given war pensions, while other veterans were given money to set up businesses or less desirable land to farm. In the North Island of New Zealand, some of the land was so isolated and rugged that the soldier-farmers walked off it. The bridge that led to this land is now called 'the Bridge to Nowhere'. The Australian system worked much better than the New Zealand system, which ended in 1922.

Over 400,000 Australians and 103,000 New Zealanders went to war; 58,961 Australians and 18,500 New Zealanders were killed. Over 64 per cent of all Australians involved and 58.6 per cent of New Zealanders were either wounded or killed. This was 6.8 per cent of Australia's population and 8.9 per cent of New Zealand's. It was a devastating blow to families and to the small populations of both countries. Memorials and monuments were erected in towns and cities. Many family members never recovered from the grief of losing their son, brother, father or husband, and others had to live with the changed or broken men who returned.

With little understanding of what the Diggers had gone through—few talked about their experiences—many civilians expected the returned soldiers to fit back in perfectly, hold down jobs and lead steady lives. Over 80,000 Australians who returned had to cope with ongoing sicknesses, while 1020 New Zealanders had lost limbs. One-armed men were taught shorthand; legless men learned to 'repair boots, class wool, and other tasks'. Those who'd experienced gas poisoning continued to suffer, and many were forced to give up office jobs to work in the outdoors. Even so, many died from the effects 10 or 20 years later.

REMEMBERING

The Diggers were haunted by memories. Some of the men lay awake night after night, thinking over things they should have done, or things they shouldn't have. Again, in their minds, they saw mates killed and maimed and listened to wounded comrades calling to them in agony from no-man's-land. They relived the sight of helpless prisoners being lined up and shot, men curling up to die or having their heads battered in with rifle butts. They remembered picking up pieces of human beings and putting them in sandbags, or burning corpses close to trenches to get rid of the smell.

Lieutenant Colonel Lawrence Blyth had enlisted after one of his brothers wrote from Egypt telling him that every man would be needed. That brother died one month before the end of the war. Another brother

> came back, having lost an arm, and he had this

> claustrophobia. He couldn't stay in a confined place or anything like that. He couldn't go into the lift, he couldn't go in the car. He couldn't do anything like that and he couldn't get any relief, so what did he do? He met up with his old cobbers and he went on the drink. He got drink, it carried him through. It helped him through.

There was little understanding of, or support for, shell-shock victims, who were generally considered to be lazy or faking their symptoms to get a war pension. When money ran out, especially during the Great Depression of the 1930s, veterans, some limbless, sang for a living on the streets, or begged with signs hung around their necks listing the battles they'd fought in. One Australian veteran wrote a song that became popular with others who'd experienced the war. It ended: 'Civvie life's a bleedin' failure, I was happy yesterday.' Some sought out the company of other veterans; some drank to dull the memories; others buried themselves in their families and work and never spoke about the war again.

But the pain was too much for some, and they ended their lives. Brigadier General 'Pompey' Elliott, the Australian commander who had helped recapture Villers-Bretonneux and had wept at the sight of his men after the Battle of Fromelles, committed suicide in 1931.

Queenslander Private Douglas Grant struggled to fit in on his return. He was one of 400 to 500 Indigenous Australians who'd served in the Great War, even though, at the time, they were not classed as Australian citizens and volunteering was no easy feat—government regulations meant Aborigines had to seek permission to leave the country. He'd tried to enlist twice before being accepted, was captured at Bullecourt in 1917 and spent the rest of the war as a POW. Fellow prisoners put him in charge of handing out the relief parcels because, according to a German, he was honest, had a quick mind, and 'was so aggressively Australian'. But if he or other Aboriginal soldiers hoped their sacrifice would earn them greater respect and equality back home, they were disappointed. Grant experienced continued racism and exclusion, and, after trying to participate in ex-servicemen's organisations, he became frustrated and disillusioned and turned to drink.

NEVER FORGET

In Belgium and France, the locals faced another harsh winter, living in ruins or shacks made from war scrap. Their fields were strewn with barbed wire and pockmarked with craters filled with stagnant, gas-poisoned water. There were many dead bodies, and unexploded shells that killed and maimed many of those who painstakingly returned the land to farming. Even today, shells ploughed up during the 'iron harvest' are left at the side of the road for collection. Remains of bodies, too, are still found.

Large memorials were erected—the memorial at Menin Gate, Ypres, records the names of 54,900 of the 'missing', while the Thiepval Memorial is inscribed with the names of 72,000 soldiers who have no known grave, mainly those killed between July and November 1916. The buried were dug up and moved to large cemeteries. Australian families were given the opportunity to write an inscription for their loved one's headstone. They ranged from 'I gave my son, he gave his life for Australia and Empire' and 'It is men, of my age and single, who are expected to do their duty' to 'Beloved only son' and 'Rest here in peace, your parents' hearts are broken, mum and dad'. The New Zealand headstones, like the British, gave the soldier's name and battalion, or, if unknown, simply the words 'A soldier of the Great War. Known unto God.'

The French and Belgian people promised to remember the Australians and New Zealanders who'd died on their soil. They erected plaques and renamed streets in Villers-Bretonneux with names like Melbourne Street, and streets in Le Quesnoy with names like Aotearoa Avenue and Place de All Blacks. School classrooms in Villers-Bretonneux still display signs with the words 'Never forget Australia.'

A NEW BEGINNING

The terms of the armistice were harsh. The Ottoman Empire was broken up, and France and Britain gained control of oil-rich countries like Iraq. The continuing wars and conflicts in the Middle East can be linked back to the splitting up of the Ottoman Empire after the war to end all wars.

Germany was forced to pay reparations to the Allies for the cost of their war effort and the ongoing expenses of their veterans and war widows. It was also occupied; vast quantities of war materials were given to the victors; and the naval blockade that had starved the German people continued. For many ordinary Germans, life after the war remained a daily struggle against hunger and poverty.

Many soldiers and politicians believed that Germany was treated too harshly—the British prime minister commented that the treaty was 'all a great pity. We shall have to do the same thing all over again in 25 years.' The Germans felt they were being unfairly punished and humiliated. As they struggled to pay back the heavy reparations to the British and French, a German veteran of the Great War who had been at Fromelles on 19 July 1916 rose to power on a wave of bitterness and nationalism. The Germans, under Adolf Hitler's Nazi Party, would once more march against the Russians, through the old Ottoman Empire and France, all the way to the coast that they had been unable to reach in the Great War. When Britain, France, New Zealand and Australia declared war on Germany again, on 3 September 1939, veterans of the Great War had no illusions about what the next generation of young men would face. Ormond Burton, a veteran-turned-pacifist, was jailed for speaking out against the Second World War as transports sailed again to Egypt in January 1940.

TIMELINE

1914

JUNE 28	Archduke Franz Ferdinand assassinated
JULY 28	Austria–Hungary declares war on Serbia
	Russia begins mobilising its army
AUGUST 1–3	Germany declares war on Russia and France
AUGUST 4	Germany invades Belgium
	Britain declares war on Germany
AUGUST 5	New Zealand and Australia declare war on Germany
AUGUST 7	First British troops land in France
AUGUST 23	Battle of Mons
SEPTEMBER 5–12	First Battle of Marne
OCTOBER 14 – NOVEMBER 22	First Battle of Ypres
OCTOBER 16	New Zealanders leave for war
OCTOBER 29	Ottoman Empire (Turkey) sides with Germany
NOVEMBER 1	Anzac convoy leaves Albany
NOVEMBER 5	Britain and France declare war on Turkey
NOVEMBER 9	HMAS *Sydney* sinks SMS *Emden*
DECEMBER 3	Anzacs reach Egypt

1915

FEBRUARY 18 - MAY 4 1916	Unrestricted German submarine campaign
APRIL 22 - MAY 25	Second Battle of Ypres
APRIL 25	Anzacs land at Gallipoli
MAY 7	*Lusitania* sunk
SEPTEMBER 25 - NOVEMBER 6	Allied offensive at Loos
DECEMBER 15	Douglas Haig replaces John French
DECEMBER 19-20	Anzacs evacuate Gallipoli

1916

JANUARY 24	Britain introduces conscription
FEBRUARY 21 - DECEMBER 18	Battle of Verdun
MARCH-MAY	Anzacs corps reach France
MAY 31 - JUNE 1	The naval Battle of Jutland
JULY 1 - NOVEMBER 17	Battle of the Somme
JULY 19-20	Battle of Fromelles
JULY 23 - SEPTEMBER 5	Battle for Pozières and Mouquet Farm
SEPTEMBER 15	Battle of Flers-Courcelette
OCTOBER 28	First Australian referendum on conscription
NOVEMBER	New Zealand begins conscription

1917

JANUARY 31	Germany announces return to unrestricted submarine warfare
FEBRUARY 21	Germans withdraw to the Hindenburg Line
APRIL 6	United States joins war
APRIL 9 - MAY 16	Battle of Arras
APRIL 11	First Battle of Bullecourt
APRIL 16	Second Battle of Aisne triggers French mutinies
MAY 3–17	Second Battle of Bullecourt
JUNE 7	Battle of Messines
JULY 31 - NOVEMBER 10	Third Battle of Ypres
SEPTEMBER 20	Battle of Menin Road
SEPTEMBER 26	Battle of Polygon Wood
OCTOBER 4	Battle of Broodseinde
OCTOBER 9	Battle of Poelcappelle
OCTOBER 12	Battle of Passchendaele
OCTOBER 26 - NOVEMBER 10	Passchendaele captured
NOVEMBER 20	Battle of Cambrai
DECEMBER 20	Second Australian referendum on conscription

1918

MARCH 3	Russia and Germany make peace

MARCH 21 - APRIL 5	German Spring Offensive
APRIL 9 - MAY 8	German Operation Georgette
APRIL 24–25	Australians recapture Villers-Bretonneux
MAY 27–30	Third stage of German Spring Offensive
JUNE 4	Battle of Le Hamel
JULY 15–19	Final stage of German Spring Offensive
AUGUST 8 - SEPTEMBER 4	Allied Hundred Days Offensive
AUGUST 31 - SEPTEMBER 3	Allied troops capture Mont St. Quentin and Péronne
SEPTEMBER 12–18	Battle of Havrincourt-Epehy
SEPTEMBER 27 - OCTOBER 1	Allied troops pierce Hindenburg Line
OCTOBER 5	Allied troops capture Montbrehain village
OCTOBER 7 - NOVEMBER 11	Last joint Allied offensive
OCTOBER 30	Turkey signs armistice
NOVEMBER 3	Austria–Hungary signs armistice
NOVEMBER 4	New Zealanders capture Le Quesnoy
NOVEMBER 11	Germany signs armistice
DECEMBER 20	New Zealanders join occupation of Germany

GLOSSARY

5.9s: 5.9-inch (150-millimetre) German shells fired high in the air from a short gun called a field howitzer.

AIF: Australian Imperial Force—a voluntary army established to fight in the Great War.

Allies: an alliance of nations joined together for a common cause, used here to refer to the alliance between countries including: Britain, France, Russia, Australia, New Zealand, Canada, India, the United States and Italy.

Artillery: transportable, mounted guns that fire shells across long distances.

Billet: a private building used as living quarters for soldiers.

Breastworks: a temporary wall made from filled sandbags or wood, used to provide cover and defence.

Cavalry: a highly mobile branch of the army that attacks on horseback.

Concussion (shock) wave: a wave of air, usually from an explosion, that is so forceful it can kill.

Conscription: compulsory enrolment in the armed forces.

Court-martialled: tried by a military court.

Duckboards: a wooden boardwalk laid over muddy ground.

Fire steps: steps or ledges cut into the inside of a trench wall to allow defenders to look out or fire.

Flank: the left or right end of an army line.

Fly-blown: crawling with maggots.

Kaiser: a German title meaning emperor.

Loopholes: a small hole through a sandbag wall or pillbox, often made of metal tubing, which allows troops to observe or shoot in safety.

NZEF: New Zealand Expeditionary Force—a voluntary army established to fight in the Great War.

Pacifist: a person who is opposed to war or violence.

Parapet: a wall of sandbags at the top of a trench, used to give protection.

Puttee: a long strip of cloth wound around the leg from ankle to knee, over clothing and boots, to give protection and support.

Ramparts: a type of defensive wall.

Referendum: a democratic process in which the public votes directly to decide a political issue.

Salient: a place in the front-line where the trenches jut out to form a bulge into enemy territory, meaning that it is surrounded by the enemy on three sides.

Sap: a deep, narrow trench that allows safe movement of troops.

Shell-shock: a nervous or mental disorder brought on by the strain of war.

Shirker: a person who tries to evade military service or work.

Skipper: an affectionate nickname for an officer.

Stokes Mortar: a rapid-firing, short-barrelled gun that fires shells at high elevations across a short range.

Storm/shock troops: soldiers that are either specially trained or intended to lead an attack.

Two-up: a gambling game in which two coins are thrown in the air and bets are laid on whether they will land head or tails.

Victoria Cross (VC): the highest British and Commonwealth medal, awarded for valour.

Very lights: a flare fired from a Very pistol, used for illumination or signalling.

WESTERN FRONT COMMANDERS

ALLIED

GENERAL SIR WILLIAM BIRDWOOD: British commander of I Anzac Corps from February 1916 to May 1918, when he was promoted to command the British 5th Army.

SIR WINSTON CHURCHILL: British officer and First Lord of the Admiralty at the start of the Great War. Demoted after the failed Gallipoli campaign, he briefly commanded a battalion on the Western Front in 1915. He returned to England in 1916, becoming minister of Munitions the following year.

BRIGADIER GENERAL HAROLD 'POMPEY' ELLIOTT: Australian commander of the 15th Brigade from March 1916 to 1919.

FIELD MARSHAL FERDINAND FOCH: French general appointed as the supreme commander of the Allied armies on the Western Front in March 1918.

FIELD MARSHAL SIR JOHN FRENCH: commander of the British Expeditionary Force from the start of the war until December 1915.

LIEUTENANT GENERAL SIR ALEXANDER GODLEY: British officer who commanded II Anzac Corps from March 1916 until the end of the war.

GENERAL SIR HUBERT GOUGH: officer in charge of the British Reserve Army (renamed the 5th Army) from July 1916 to May 1918.

FIELD MARSHAL SIR DOUGLAS HAIG: war general and commander-in-chief of the British Expeditionary Force, including the AIF and NZEF, from December 1915 until the end of the war.

GENERAL SIR RICHARD HAKING: British officer who commanded a brigade, then a division and subsequently XI Corps from September 1915 to the end of the war.

GENERAL JOSEPH JOFFRE: commander-in-chief of the French Army from 1914 to 1916.

LIEUTENANT GENERAL SIR JAMES MCCAY: commander of the 5th Australian Division from July 1916 to January 1917.

LIEUTENANT GENERAL JOHN MONASH: commander of the 3rd Australian Division from December 1916 to May 1918, when he was given command of the Australian Corps.

GENERAL ROBERT NIVELLE: commander-in-chief of the French Army from December 1916 to May 1917.

GENERAL JOHN PERSHING: commander of the American Expeditionary Forces from May 1917 to the end of the war.

GENERAL HENRI-PHILIPPE PÉTAIN: general who first commanded a division, then a corps and then an army before becoming commander-in-chief of the French Army in May 1917.

GENERAL SIR HERBERT PLUMER: affectionately known as 'old Plum' or 'Daddy Plumer' to his men, commander of the British 2nd Army in Flanders from May 1915 to the end of the war.

MAJOR GENERAL SIR ANDREW RUSSELL: commander of the New Zealand Division from March 1916 to the end of the war.

LIEUTENANT GENERAL SIR HAROLD WALKER: British general who commanded the 1st Australian Division from April 1916 to July 1918.

GERMAN

GENERAL ERICH VON FALKENHAYN: commander of the German Army from 1914 to 1916.

FIELD MARSHAL PAUL VON HINDENBURG: commander-in-chief of the German Army from 1916 to 1919.

FIRST QUARTERMASTER GENERAL ERICH VON LUDENDORFF: joint war-leader of the German Army from 1916 to 1918.

ACKNOWLEDGMENTS

ZERO HOUR was only possible because of the dedication of earlier and contemporary historians, particularly the official Australian historian Charles Bean. Thanks to Les Cleveland, Harry Ricketts and Ian McGibbon for their assistance with the poems. Ali Arnold, my editor, has once again worked tirelessly to give this story life, and Clare Moleta, my partner, has given invaluable feedback and support. Thanks to everyone at Text Publishing for making *Zero Hour* the best it could be.

Text Publishing would like to thank the Australian War Memorial for their advice and comments on the manuscript, particularly Robert Nichols. Many thanks to historian Brad Manera for his fact-checking and careful reading of the manuscript.

BIBLIOGRAPHY

Adam-Smith, Patsy. *The Anzacs.* Hamish Hamilton, 1978.

Aitken, Alexander. *Gallipoli to the Somme: recollections of a New Zealand infantryman.* Oxford University Press, 1963.

Baker, Paul. *King and country call: New Zealanders, conscription and the Great War.* Auckland University Press, 1988.

Baxter, Archibald. *We will not cease.* Penguin, 1980.

Bean, C. E. W. *The Australian Imperial Force in France, 1916.* Official history of Australia in the war of 1914–1918, vol. III, 12th edn. Angus & Robertson, 1941.

———*The Australian Imperial Force in France, 1917.* Official history of Australia in the war of 1914–1918, vol. IV, 11th edn. Angus & Robertson, 1941.

———*The Australian Imperial Force in France during the main German offensive, 1918.* Official history of Australia in the war of 1914–1918, vol. V, 8th edn. Angus & Robertson, 1941.

———*The Australian Imperial Force in France during the Allied offensive, 1918.* Official history of Australia in the war of 1914–1918, vol. VI, 1st edn. Angus & Robertson, 1942.

———*Anzac to Amiens.* Australian War Memorial, 1983.

Boyack, Nicholas. *Behind the lines: the lives of New Zealand soldiers in the First World War.* Allen & Unwin/Port Nicholson Press, 1989.

Boyack, Nicholas & Jane Tolerton. *In the shadow of war: New Zealand soldiers talk about World War One and their lives.* Penguin, 1990.

Bromby, Robin. *German raiders of the South Seas: the naval threat to Australia/New Zealand 1914–17.* Doubleday, 1985.

Burton, Ormond. *The silent division.* Angus & Robertson, 1935.

Byrne, A. E. *Official history of the Otago Regiment, N.Z.E.F. in the Great War, 1914–1918.* Wilkie & Co., 1921.

Carlyon, Les. *The Great War.* Pan Macmillan, 2006.

Carthew, Noel. *Voices from the trenches: letters to home.* New Holland, 2002.

Cochrane, Peter. *The Western Front: 1916–1920.* ABC Books, 2001.

Cutlack, F. M. *The Australian Flying Corps in the western and eastern theatres of war, 1914–1918.* Official history of Australia in the war of 1914–1918, vol. VIII, 11th edn. Angus & Robertson, 1941.

Dennis, Peter, Jeffrey Grey, Ewan Morris & Robin Prior, *The Oxford companion to Australian military history.* 2nd edn. Oxford University Press, 2008.

Downing, W. H. *To the last ridge: the World War One experiences of W. H. Downing.* Grub Street, 2005.

Gammage, Bill. *The broken years: Australian soldiers in the Great War.* Australian National University Press, 1974.

Harper, Glyn. *Dark journey: three key New Zealand battles of the Western Front.* HarperCollins, 2007.

Harper, Glyn (ed.). *Letters from the battlefield: New Zealand soldiers write home, 1914–18.* HarperCollins, 2001.

Holt, Tonie & Valmai. *Battlefields of the First World War: a traveller's guide.* Pavilion, 1993.

Howard, Michael. *The First World War.* Oxford University Press, 2002.

Ingram, N. M. *Anzac diary: a nonentity in khaki.* Treharne, 1987.

Jünger, Ernst. *Storm of steel.* Penguin, 2004.

King, Melve (comp. Neil Frances & Doug King). *Things have been pretty lively: the Great War diary of Melve King.* Wairarapa Archive/Fraser Books, 2008.

Lee, A. *Soldier.* A. H. & A. W. Reed, 1976.

Macdonald, Andrew. *On my way to the Somme: New Zealanders and the bloody offensive of 1916.* HarperCollins, 2005.

MacKenzie, Clutha (ed.). *Chronicles of NZEF,* vol. I, no. 3, 29 September 1916; vol. II, no. 15, 28 March 1917; vol. IV, no. 45, 7 June 1918; vol. V, no. 56, 8 November 1918.

Malthus, Cecil. *Armentères and the Somme,* Reed Publishing, 2002

Marriot, Allan. *Mud beneath my boots: a poignant memoir of the effects of war on a young New Zealander.* HarperCollins, 2005.

Mitchell, G. D. *Backs to the wall.* Angus & Robertson, 1937.

Neiberg, Michael S. *The Western Front 1914–1916: from the Schlieffen Plan to Verdun and the Somme.* The history of World War I. Amber Books, 2008.

——*The Western Front 1917–1918: from Vimy Ridge to Amiens and the armistice.* The history of World War I. Amber Books, 2008.

Pederson, Peter. *The Anzacs. Gallipoli to the Western Front.* Viking, 2007.

Pelvin, Richard (ed.). *Anzac: an illustrated history 1914–1918.* Hardie Grant, 2004.

Phillips, Jock, Nicholas Boyack & E. P. Malone (eds). *The great adventure: New Zealand soldiers describe the First World War.* Allen & Unwin/Port Nicholson Press, 1988.

Pugsley, Christopher. *On the fringe of hell: New Zealanders and military discipline in the First World War.* Hodder & Stoughton, 1991.

Sassoon, Siegfried. *The war poems of Siegfried Sassoon.* Faber & Faber, 1983.

Scott, Ernest. *Australia during the war.* Official history of Australia in the war of 1914–1918, volume XI, 7th edn. Angus & Robertson, 1941.

Sievers, Gerald. *World War One diary of Gerald Sievers.* Unpublished: private collection of Patricia Lissienko.

Silkin, Jon (ed.). *The Penguin book of First World War poetry.* Penguin, 1979.

Stewart, H. *Official history of New Zealand's effort in the Great War.* Whitcombe & Tombe, 1921.

Stinton, Harry (ed. Virginia Mayo). *Harry's war: a British Tommy's experiences in the trenches in World War One.* Conway, 2002.

Strachan, Hew. *The First World War.* Simon & Schuster, 2003.

Tolerton, Jane. *Ettie: a life of Ettie Rout.* Penguin, 1992.

Treadwell, C. A. L. *Recollections of an amateur soldier.* Thomas Avery & Sons, 1936.

Williams, E. P. *A New Zealander's diary: Gallipoli and France 1915–1917.* Cadsonbury Publications, 1998.

Williams, H. R. *The gallant company: an Australian soldier's story of 1915–1918.* Angus & Robertson, 1933.

Wilson, Patrick (ed.). *So far from home: the remarkable diaries of Eric Evans, an Australian soldier during World War I.* Kangaroo Press, 2002.

Wright, Matthew. *Western Front: the New Zealand Division in the First World War, 1916–18.* Reed Publishing, 2005.

WEBSITES

www.cambridgeairforce.org.nz

www.naa.gov.au

www.nzfpm.co.nz

www.nzhistory.net.nz

www.awm.gov.au

www.nzetc.org

www.dva.gov.au

www.cwgc.org

www.aucklandmuseum.com

REFERENCES

Footage

To see footage taken at the Somme River mentioned on page 188, visit: http://www.youtube.com/watch?v=3bggGLzk6cQ

Also see: http://www.ww1westernfront.gov.au/heath-cemetery/video.html http://aso.gov.au/titles/documentaries/australia-world-war-1/clip1/

Introduction

'I personally feel...' quoted in Boyack & Tolerton, pages 47–8

Chapter 1

'I wouldn't have missed...' quoted in E. P. Williams, page 267

'the last man and last shilling', quoted in Bean, *Anzac to Amiens*, page 23

'The lamps are going...' quoted in Wilson, page 2

'good fellows', quoted in Sievers

'to death', quoted in Bean, *Anzac to Amiens*, page 213

Chapter 2

'BLAKE—Killed in action...' posted in *The Age*, 19 July 1917

'It is an immense relief...' quoted in Boyack, page 66

'quite happy now that...' quoted in Phillips, Boyack & Malone, page 268

'has to run like blazes...' quoted in Phillips, Boyack & Malone, page 268

'The front line is rather like heaven...' quoted in Malthus, page 38

'the big-looked-forward-to day...' quoted in Gammage, page 149

'Australians go home...' quoted in Bean, Vol. III, page 194

'about six seconds after the explosion...' quoted in Pugsley, page 68

'and is hopful', quoted in Bean, Vol. III, page 265

'worked up...' quoted in Bean, Vol. III, page 347

'Advance Australia...' quoted in Pederson, page 128

'cried like a child', quoted in Gammage, page 158

'You won't find a German...' quoted in Bean, Vol. III, page 362 'looked over the top, they saw…' quoted in Bean, Vol. III, page 358

'but more terrible, more…' quoted in Downing, page 11

'wounded and dying men…' quoted in Bean, Vol. III, page 383

'blurred by dust…' quoted in Bean, Vol. III, page 417

'in the air at a time', quoted in Bean, Vol. III, page 420

'wounded could be seen …' quoted in Bean, Vol. III, page 437

'perhaps for the last time…' quoted in Gammage, page 160

'Don't forget me, cobber', quoted in Bean, Vol. III, page 441

'Stretcher-bearer!…' quoted in H. Williams, page 65

'in arm and leg…' quoted in Gammage, page 160

'were not sufficiently trained…' quoted in Bean, Vol. III, page 444

'Yesterday evening, south of…' quoted in Bean, Vol. III, page 446

'We thought we knew something…' quoted in Gammage, page 161

Chapter 3

'Nocturne' (extract), quoted in *New Zealand at the front, 1918.* Written and illustrated by men of the New Zealand Division. Cassell & Co., 1918, page 52

'I want you to go into the line…' quoted in Bean, *Anzac to Amiens,* page 293

'hasty or ill-considered', quoted in Bean, Vol. III, page 468

'The tension affected the men…' quoted in Gammage, page 162

'Hell's trenches…' quoted in Bean, Vol. III, page 522

'urgent and secret', quoted in Bean, Vol. III, page 537

'Heavy firing all morning…' quoted in Gammage, page 165

'*Gott mit uns*', quoted in Bean, Vol. III, page 599

'dug out and buried again', quoted in Bean, Vol. III, page 618

'most scientific and most military…' quoted in Bean, Vol. III, page 643

'the strain had sent two other…' quoted in Bean, Vol. III, page 658

'I have had much…' quoted in Bean, Vol. III, pages 660–1

'Huns and Aussies were…' quoted in Bean, Vol. III, page 720

'When you see this I'll be dead…' quoted in Bean, Vol. III, page 797

'All we are doing is using up…' quoted in Bean, Vol. III, page 876

'book on the life of an infantryman…' quoted in Bean, Vol. III, page 872

'Nothing published in the papers is worth…' quoted in Bean, Vol. III, page 872

'through the incompetence, callousness...' quoted in Bean, Vol. III, page 872
'marks a ridge more densely...' quoted in Bean, *Anzac to Amiens*, page 264

Chapter 4

'In Memoriam' (extract), quoted in MacKenzie, Vol.II, page 67
'The sights to be seen are terrible...' quoted in MacDonald, page 149
'The face was turned away...' quoted in MacDonald, page 152
'Finnigan', quoted in MacDonald, page 235
'Hell on the Somme', quoted in Stewart, page 101
'sandbag kilt', quoted in Pugsley, page 122
'simply Hell on earth', quoted in Harper, page 68
'not war, it's absolute murder', quoted in Harper, page 66
'mass of confused memories...' quoted in Boyack, page 74
'My God, you are going...' quoted in H. Williams, page 86
'churned to the consistency...' quoted in Mitchell, page 14
'muddy rabbits', 'howled out of foggy space...' quoted in Mitchell, page 27
'I'm not going in—I'm finished', quoted in Bean, Vol. III, page 941
'reeked so strongly of gasoline', quoted in Bean, Vol. III, page 919
'the longer a man served...' quoted in Mitchell, page 168
'some day there will be warmth...' quoted in Mitchell, page 51
'happy, hopeful, young faces', quoted in Wilson, page 60
'spirit of the bayonet', quoted in E. P. Williams, page 206
'bully beef stew, layered with ice...' quoted in Marriot, page 33

Chapter 5

'Sing me to sleep', courtesy of Les Cleveland
'Once more from the same old place...' quoted in Boyack, page 64
'very quiet, the only thing we heard...' quoted in E. P. Williams, page 212
'night crept slowly by...', 'That shut the cow up', quoted in Mitchell, page 252
'Those damn flares constantly rising...' quoted in Wilson, page 80
'some snatches of indistinct...' quoted in Malthus, page 66
'Very short of tucker yesterday...' quoted in Gammage, page 174
'like rabbits in holes...' quoted in Phillips, Boyack & Malone, page 239

'They are tireless brutes...', 'satisfaction from the popping sound...' quoted in Wilson, page 89

'best of times...' quoted in Gammage, page 152

'The yells were really pitiful...' quoted in Boyack, page 106

'example to the rest', quoted in Pugsley, page 121

'I want to see them shoot', quoted in Pugsley, page 108

'not a born soldier...' quoted in Pugsley, page 153

'should have been sent in...' quoted in MacDonald, page 237

'to shoot a boy...' quoted in Pugsley, page 211

'something in trench-holding that is...' quoted in Mitchell, page 253

'sit crouched day and night in a wet...' quoted in Pugsley, page 236

'really brave man is he who...' quoted in Pugsley, page 272

'been completely destroyed', quoted in Pugsley, page 262

'A chap said to me today as we marched...' quoted in Wilson, page 79

'It's a blighty, a good blighty...' quoted in Malthus, page 120

'No one who had actually gone...' quoted in Gammage, page 214

'vastly pleased with himself...' quoted in Mitchell, page 168

'a glorious feeling', quoted in Burton, page 229

'Though fairly old, she was still quite...', 'A simply ripping day, quite...' quoted in Wilson, page 162

'a pitiful sight to see women and children...' quoted in King, page 144

'most of the bus and tram drivers...' quoted in Pugsley, page 153

'among the old familiar faces...' quoted in Gammage, page 213

Chapter 6

'GLASSINGTON—Died of wounds...' posted in *Sydney Morning Herald*, 5 April 1919

'The Last Post is being played...' quoted on www.anzacday.org.au/history/ww1/anecdotes/casualty.html

'as long as men are available', quoted in Stewart, page 59

'What use am I if I am broken...' quoted in Baxter, page 123

'Will you send another woman's...' quoted in Scott, page 43

Don't leave the boys...' quoted on http://billyhughes.moadoph.gov.au/conscription

'murder (or near enough to it)...' quoted on http://www.samemory.sa.gov.au/site/page.cfm?u=1022

'Vote No, Mum, they'll...' quoted on www.awm.gov.au (ID number: RC00336)

Chapter 7

'NITCHIE—In loving memory...' posted in *Geelong Advertiser*, 19 July 1920

'violence, brutality and rapidity', quoted in Holt, page 84

'grape-like bunches of coloured lights', quoted in Mitchell, page 89

'like a crowd from a football match', quoted in Bean, Vol. IV, page 282

'of what use would I be tonight', quoted in Bean, Vol. IV, page 290

'seemed to swarm with fireflies', quoted in Bean, Vol. IV, page 295

'keep the position till the cows...' quoted in Bean, Vol. IV, page 317

'only describe it as Hell...' quoted in Gammge, page 183

'fight it out like Australians', quoted in Bean, Vol. IV, page 333

'run the gauntlet back through...' quoted in Bean, Vol. IV, page 334

'You are not going to leave us?', quoted in Mitchell, page 97

'Finish hospital', quoted in Bean, Vol. IV, page 341

'Bloody April', quoted in Holt, page 85

'What time is zero?', quoted in Bean, Vol. IV, page 429

'Pull out—retire—get back for your lives', quoted in Bean, Vol. IV, page 435

'the old familiar "pop..."', 'every man for himself...' quoted on www.awm.gov.au/atwar/ww1_flying.asp

'Stick it out, lad...' quoted in Bean, Vol. IV, page 484

Chapter 8

'A trench, a stench...' quoted in MacKenzie, Vol. I, page 63

'men killed alongside you...' quoted in Harper, *Letters from the Battlefield*, page 99

'It's our turn...', 'poor, frightened devils', quoted in Harper, *Letters from the Battlefield*, page 100

'Alright Sir, if it is to be taken...' quoted in Bean, Vol. IV, page 673

'Somehow we get wrong ideas...' quoted in Harper, *Letters from the Battlefield*, page 101 'make our names stand out…' quoted in Gammage, page 116

'a queer thrill shot through me…' quoted in Gammage, page 256

'felt little emotion, just intense…' quoted in Wilson, page 198

'for another smack at the…' quoted in Gammage, page 257

'but one does not think till…' quoted in Gammage, page 224

'I don't think old Fritz…' quoted in Boyack, page 92

'They are dead, and for their…' quoted in Wilson, page 118

'in a rain of flowers…', 'in an age of security…' quoted in Jünger, page 5

'No one can help…' quoted in Jünger, page 92

'a series of low long-drawn-out…' quoted in Jünger, page 98

'poor old Jim was laying there…' quoted in Boyack & Tolerton, page 39

'the sour smell of new death…' quoted in Mitchell, page 143

'You've got a decoration…' quoted in Mitchell, page 147

'occasional cry of "Stretcher-bearers!"…' quoted in Wilson, page 78

'I'm hit…' quoted in Mitchell, pages 157–8

Chapter 9

'Thoughts', quoted in MacKenzie, Vol. IV, page 203

'like a Gippsland bushfire', quoted in Bean, Vol. IV, page 813

'Old Fritz's morale vanishes…' quoted in Wilson, page 124

'It's great sport, driving them…' quoted in Wilson, page 122

'every square yard of it…' quoted in Harper, *Dark Journey*, page 40

'We are given a damn lot…' quoted in Wilson, page 126

'Of course don't forget…' quoted in Boyack & Tolerton, page 32

'We always believed we were…' quoted in Adam-Smith, page 311

'pipe up like the Aussies', quoted in Tolerton, page 140

'stern, dour and grim', quoted in Stewart, page 616

'crump, crump', quoted in Bean, *Anzac to Amiens*, page 370

'Dear M, D and G…' quoted in Phillips, Boyack & Malone, page 127

'a pig's life, humans were…' quoted in Ingram, page 55

'that there should be no postponement…' quoted in Bean, Vol. IV, page 884

'as dry as a bone', quoted in Bean, Vol. IV, page 884

'The official attitude is that…' quoted in Bean, Vol. IV, page 884 'flesh and blood…' quoted in Bean, Vol. IV, page 908

'Stretcher bearer…' quoted in Phillips, Boyack & Malone, page 148

'one pillbox to find it just…' quoted in Bean, Vol. IV, page 906

'I have seen some pretty…' quoted in Phillips, Boyack & Malone, page 148

'a pretty dumb beast…' quoted in Boyack & Tolerton, page 32

'I do not feel as confident…' quoted in Stewart, page 292

'Most gratifyingly…' quoted in Bean, Vol. IV, page 928

'what am I to do?', quoted in Bean, Vol. IV, page 918

'the stunt should never have…' quoted in Harper, *Dark Journey*, page 87

'the bloody heads…' quoted in Harper, *Letters from the Battlefield*, page 114

'cold driving rain and hail', quoted in Stewart, page 293

'the agony was awful…' quoted in Harper, *Letters from the Battlefield*, page 120

'we couldn't find him…' quoted on http://www.nzhistory.net.nz/media/sound/sidney-stanfield-remembers-passchendaele

'flew incredible distances', quoted in Jünger, page 319

Chapter 10

'BIRD—In loving memory…' posted in *Sydney Morning Herald*, 1 September 1919

'Get out of the road…' quoted in Gammage, page 209

'get killed', quoted in Harper, *Dark Journey*, page 206

'It was the only time I used…' quoted in Harper, *Dark Journey*, page 224

'sent another lot and he got…' quoted in Harper, *Dark Journey*, page 240

'Who are you?', quoted in Bean, Vol. V, page 172

'hold on at all costs', quoted in Bean, Vol. V, page 321

'Goodbye, boys, it's neck or nothing', quoted in Bean, Vol. V, page 340

'Australians', quoted in Bean, Vol. V, page 397

'Here lies a brave English…' quoted in Bean, Vol. V, page 418

'Every position must be held…' quoted in Bean, Vol. V, page 437

'like firing at a whole haystack…' quoted in Bean, Vol. V, page 467

'for two days companies of infantry…' quoted in Bean, Vol. V, page 540

'If it was God-Almighty…' quoted in Bean, Vol. V, page 575

'Kill every bloody German…' quoted in Bean, Vol. V, page 580

'New waves always come on...' quoted in Bean, Vol. V, page 590

'It's Anzac Day...' quoted in Downing, page 117

'There they go...' quoted in Downing, page 119

'War hardened as I was...' quoted in Mitchell, page 211

'untrained rabble', quoted in Mitchell, page 216

'with a voice like a bull', quoted in Bean, Vol. V, page 650

'Surrender be—...' quoted in Bean, Vol. V, page 653

Chapter 11

'LINFORD—In sad and loving memory...' posted in *The Argus*, 6 October 1919

'We have the Australians opposite...' quoted in Bean, Vol. VI, page 59

'They lay opposite us, exceptionally...' quoted in Bean, Vol. VI, page 60

'good assault division...' quoted in Stewart, page 618

'a complete battalion had been wiped out', quoted in Bean, Vol. VI, page 240

'They're not Americans...' quoted in Treadwell, page 213

'keep your mouths shut', quoted in Stewart, page 418

'being behind a curtain...' quoted in Bean, Vol. VI, page 531

'a wonderful sound...' quoted in Harper, *Dark Journey*, page 361

'everything is lost', quoted in Bean, Vol. VI, page 614

'sure he did not know...' quoted in Harper, *Dark Journey*, page 442

'lot of bushrangers', quoted in Bean, *Anzacs to Amiens*, page 481

'it all happened like...' quoted in Bean, *Anzacs to Amiens*, page 482

'burnt the grass and earth black', quoted in Stewart, page 479

'one minute', quoted in Wilson, page 210

'Which way?', quoted in Bean, Vol. VI, page 906

'All I can say is you...' quoted in Bean, Vol. VI, page 926

'put in to do', quoted in Bean, Vol. VI, page 933

'recoil of thousands of guns...' quoted in Downing, page 176

'sick of the war and had...' quoted in Bean, Vol. VI, page 1036

'it was just a relief, we didn't...' quoted in Boyack & Tolerton, page 240

'everyone was so dog tired ...' quoted in Tolerton, page 188

'Fancy no more shells...' quoted in Boyack, page 88

'it all seemed unreal…' quoted in Mitchell, page 278

'The fighting is finished…' quoted in Wilson, page 227

Chapter 12

'Fern Seed' (extract), quoted in MacKenzie, Vol. V, page 177

'first to come…' quoted in Bean, Vol. VI, page 1058

'was just a soldier who'd come…' quoted in Boyack & Tolerton, page 243

'repair boots, class wool…' quoted in Lee, page 127

'came back, having lost an arm…' quoted in Boyack, page 71

'Civvie life's a bleedin' failure…' quoted in Gammage, page 271

'was so aggressively Australian', quoted in Dennis et al., page 241

'I gave my son, he gave his life…' quoted in www.dva.gov.au/commems_oawg/commemorations/education/Documents/Western_Front.pdf, page 92.

'all a great pity…' quoted in Carthew, page 238

INDEX